The French Foreign Legion

THE INSIDE STORY OF THE WORLD-FAMOUS FIGHTING FORCE

INTRODUCTION BY LEN DEIGHTON
THE HISTORY OF THE LEGION BY ERWAN BERGOT

Thames and Hudson

The
French Foreign Legion

THE INSIDE STORY OF THE WORLD-FAMOUS
FIGHTING FORCE

John Robert Young

To my beloved wife Jenny – who made it all possible.

Throughout the book, the term 'Legionnaire' denotes any member of the French Foreign Legion, irrespective of rank, while 'légionnaire' indicates the rank of private soldier. Military ranks are normally given in the French form ('capitaine', 'sergent', 'caporal', etc.). See the note under 'Equivalent Ranks' on page 209.

'The History of the Legion' translated from the French by Martin Windrow

Art Direction and Book Design by Bob Hook
First published in Great Britain in 1984
by Thames and Hudson Ltd, London

© 1984 John Robert Young
Introduction © 1984 Len Deighton
'The History of the Legion' and design © 1984 Thames and Hudson Ltd, London

Printed and bound in Italy by Arnoldo Mondadori, Verona

On the half-title: The 13th DBLE in the breakout from Bir Hakeim, 10 June 1942.

On the title page: Dawn over Camp Raffalli, Corsica, headquarters of the 2nd REP.

On this page: Lieutenant-colonel Rollet with the colour of the RMLE in 1918, flanked by four Chevaliers of the Legion of Honour from the regiment.

Contents

Allegory of the Foreign Legion in 1931. General Rollet with flags of the Legion and the Monument to the Dead.

Introduction.

LEN DEIGHTON

In our far-travelled, communication-sated, permissive society there are few remaining conversation stoppers. But any man who can say 'I served with the Legion' is guaranteed an audience. There is something intriguing about an enclosed society. It attracts our attention, arouses our curiosity and baffles by exclusion.

The Legion is an enigma, even to the French. The Legion trusts no one, and even retired veterans speak cautiously. And the Legion has its enemies. Some suspect that the Legion has political ambitions, and the Algerian revolt, in which one battalion of the Legion supported the rebels, did nothing to quell the disquiet.

For one hundred and fifty years the Legion has kept its doors tightly closed to reporters and photographers: so it is remarkable that the man who finally got inside this secret world is an Englishman.

When the Legion came up against John Robert Young, it met a man with the spirit of the Legion. He first got this idea about a photo-record of the French Foreign Legion as long ago as 1960, when he was in Algeria near that legendary home of the Legion, Sidi-bel-Abbès. This was the old headquarters of the Legion, the place where its archives were stored and its treasures cherished. One such treasure being a wooden false hand. It once belonged to the commander of a company of Legionnaires which fought to near extinction against an estimated two thousand Mexicans in April 1863. Each year the hand is paraded on Camerone Day, 30 April – the anniversary of the fight – lest any Legionnaire forget the story.

The Legion was created as a fighting force and it has known little peace. In 1945, as World War Two ended, the Legion was drawn into the fighting for Indo-China, which, punctuated by the disaster of Dien Bien Phu, eventually became the war in Vietnam.

One can't talk of the Legion without talking about its role in the Algerian fighting. The OAS (Organisation de l'Armée Secrète) was a clandestine right-wing group of colonists who wanted to keep Algeria French at all costs. In May 1958 the (French) Army in Algiers had occupied government buildings there to demand a return to power of President de Gaulle. But even de Gaulle couldn't bring back 1939, and in 1961 the army staged another revolt to support French control in Algeria. When the dust settled, three French army units, including the 1st Foreign Parachute Regiment, were disbanded because of the part they'd played in the revolt. This gives a piquancy to the photo of the Legionnaires drinking cold beer in the general store under a portrait of General de Gaulle. For the Legionnaires, de Gaulle occupies a special place in their history.

In 1962 Algeria was granted independence after a long, bitter struggle which split France and is still not forgotten by either side. The Legion moved to mainland France and Corsica. To some it seemed as if the Legion was going into decline. In any case it seemed as if there was little chance of a story such as the one John Robert Young wanted to do. But Young is a veteran photo-journalist, an enthusiast who doesn't take no for an answer. Who else would write a letter to the President of the Republic? Who else would get a reply that opened doors that had stayed so long shut?

I've known John Robert Young since the late sixties. He is a dedicated man, and to hear him talk about the Legion is to understand how nothing could stop him completing this project. He has given a large chunk of his life to making this amazing record, and financed it himself. That sincerity is apparent in every picture he took. And yet his devotion to making a truthful record is such that he will not pose or arrange pictures or even plan them. There is a simple honesty in every picture he has taken. This not only provides a unique record of the Legion, it gained for him the Legion's friendship and trust, which was a necessary part of the project.

Since that permission arrived from the Elysée Palace, John has travelled thousands of miles to be with the Legion. Equipped with his cameras, and always carrying (literally) hundreds of rolls of film and his tiny Pearlcorder tape recorder, he made a superb record of those moments we've all envisioned. At Aubagne, the headquarters of the Legion, he photographed and spoke with young recruits as they signed their contracts.

Young was the first photo-journalist accredited to the Legion and permitted to document the daily life of the men for an illustrated book. Until this, even the Legion mess halls and the soldiers eating lunch had been closed to outsiders, and especially to journalists and photographers. Young started at the beginning. He followed a batch of recruits to their preliminary training camp at Castelnaudary. All the time showing his eye for the human touch. What a wonderful photograph he has of the young Legionnaire at Mass.

And for those whose French is not good enough, the Legion provides language classes. At one time no language allowances were made for the foreign recruit, but even in the Legion things are getting a little easier.

Over Corsica he flew in the troop carriers of the Legion's 2nd Parachute Regiment. Some of these men took part in the raid that rescued the European families from Kolwezi in Zaïre when it seemed that they would be massacred by the guerrillas.

At Corte, Corsica, he climbed with men of the Legion's mountain section. He went to the Commando School in the Pyrenees to see Legionnaires in a training programme that included chopping their way through ice-topped water. The photos are enough to give you pneumonia.

But if the photos of hardship are so telling, so are the pictures of Legionnaires off duty, and the pictures of the Legionnaires with their families. Particularly good were the shots taken in the veteran home at Puyloubier, where old men make wine and ceramics. And the veterans who come on parade each year and for one day wear the white képi.

As might be expected of a formation that consists mostly of men far away from their birthplace and their homes and families, Christmas is a cherished celebration. Young spent Christmas at Orange in southern France with the Legion's 1st Cavalry Regiment. At this time the Legion has an old tradition of officers presenting every Legionnaire with a personal gift. Over Christmas Young met one of the few women ever admitted into the Legion. One of these women, La Comtesse Ladislas du Luart – known as 'Marraine' ('Godmother') to everyone in the Regiment – was with the Legion in World War Two. She wears more medals than the Colonel of the Regiment.

I asked John what was the most memorable moment of the time he'd spent with the Legion. I expected some frightening experience in the jungle, or some danger in the mountains or some account of hardship or fear. Instead, he told me that it was in the small hours of the morning during this Christmas with the Legion, as he heard the massed voices singing the Legion's old songs.

Thousands of miles away from Orange, Young found himself cutting his way through the rain forest of French Guiana. The Legion patrols the Brazil border and protects the European rocket facilities. Look seaward and you can see the silhouette of Devil's Island. No talk of desertion here; no one has ever succeeded in getting through the jungle alive. All this time John Robert Young lived the hard life of a Legionnaire. They gave him Legionnaire's clothing and equipment complete with combat jacket with the name tab YOUNG: all was ready and waiting. He slept in the jungle, ate Legion rations (and sometimes wild boar), and listened to the small talk and continued taking superb photos.

Keeping photo equipment clean and working in jungle conditions is no easy matter. All his professional skills were needed when he went on a river patrol. The thirty-man patrol used 'pirogues', primitive local canoes. These are the only craft suited to the narrows, the rocks and the rapids, and to the difficulties of hauling all the guns, fuel, food and equipment, as well as the boats, through the jungle past those stretches of the Oyapock River which are not navigable.

Perhaps it is appropriate that John Robert Young, an Englishman, should have been the first man to record the inside story of the Legion, for it still retains its role as the *Légion Etrangère* and gives shelter to more than a hundred nationalities. There are plenty of other Englishmen in the ranks. Any fiction writer would envy John as he finds such wonderful characters as 'King', who speaks French mixed with Liverpudlian dialect, and, like his friend 'Heinz', shapes his jungle hat in cowboy style. And what about the mysterious 'Ranji Singh', the pharmacy student from Bengal, who is saving up to buy a house in France? The Legion guarantees its recruits their anonymity. And the Legion takes that guarantee seriously. All Legionnaires likely to be within range of Young's lenses were warned, and given a chance to avoid his cameras and his questions.

It is the rankers of the Legion that give it a large measure of the curious mystique. The faces in the photos are the faces of men with stories to tell. In the Legion have been found doctors, professors, bishops and princes. It is the pride of the Legion that they don't call in experts from outside. They have experts of every sort serving in their ranks. The Legion officers are virtually all on attachment from other regiments of the French Army, but serving with the Legion is a matter of pride. Officers returning to their regiments continue to wear one Legion button on their tunic to identify them as men who served with that small élite.

The Legion is demanding; the work is tough and its punishments are hard. The old stories about men buried up to the neck in sand are not the inventions of some Hollywood hack. Even now the Legion has its own justice and life is harsh for those unwilling to accept the Legion's ways. But the Legion is more than just a military formation and it has survived because it provides not just a home and family but a new life and a new country. The Legionnaire is not merely a civilian who becomes a soldier. He is an immigrant and exile. For many Legionnaires, leave has no attraction and no meaning.

The Legion is a secret world, and is jealous of that secrecy. There is no doubt that the Legion recognized in John Robert Young a fellow spirit. In fact one Legionnaire eventually confided, 'No matter what authority you had from Paris, if the Legion didn't like you, you wouldn't be here'.

The History of the Legion.

ERWAN BERGOT

The Law of 9 March 1831, authorizing the formation of the Foreign Legion.

Louis-Philippe, King of the French,
To all present and to come, Greeting.
In view of the Law of 9 March 1831;
On the report of our Secretary
of State at the Department of War;
We have commanded and do
command as follows:

ARTICLE 1
There will be formed a Legion
composed of Foreigners.
This Legion will take the name of
Foreign Legion.

So begins the royal ordinance of 10 March 1831, the true 'birth certificate' of the French Foreign Legion. On putting his signature to it, Louis-Philippe can hardly have imagined what lay ahead for this élite unit, destined to become legendary the world over. In sober fact, he had taken this step simply in the hope of strengthening his hold on the throne.

On that March day in 1831, what could come to be called the 'July Monarchy' had existed for only seven months, since the revolution of 25 July 1830 that had driven King Charles X into exile in England. The new regime did not lack enemies. There were the 'Legitimists' of the Bourbon party, who considered Louis-Philippe of Orleans a usurper, and who remembered that in 1793 his father, 'Philippe Egalité', had condoned the execution of his cousin Louis XVI. There were former Bonapartists, who had rallied to Louis XVIII in 1815. And there were republicans, who felt robbed of their revolution by this 'bourgeois' monarchy.

Louis-Philippe's accession had been followed – as always in France – by a 'reorganization', which was no more than a purge of adherents of the old regime in favour of the partisans of the new. The army did not escape this process. The creation of the Foreign Legion (which Marshal Soult, the Minister of War, decreed 'should not be employed in the continental territory of the kingdom') was intended to remove from France those officers and soldiers, French or foreign, who were felt to be awkward, excitable or frankly dangerous subjects for the new monarchy.

It was a stroke of luck for Louis-Philippe that Charles X had left him, among other legacies, a year-old war in Algeria; Algiers itself had fallen to the French only days before the July Revolution. This good fortune provided, for the young Legion and for other restless units which would later form the 'Army of Africa', a distant arena in which they could work off that energy which, on the soil of France, might imperil the throne of a king whose inclinations were bourgeois and pacifist.

The officers around whom the Legion was formed were drawn in part from among those who had formerly served in Napoleon's Grande Armée and who had been rotting on half-pay since 1815. The mass of the recruits were from European nations, driven to abandon their homelands either by political turmoil (as in the case of Italians, Spaniards and Poles), or by economic hardship (the Swiss), or by both together (as with the Belgians and Dutch). There were also a number of Frenchmen, some tempted by the chance of battle and adventure in exotic surroundings, and others who were simply anxious to put a certain distance between themselves and the law.

THE LEGION'S ANCESTORS

This was not the first time that France had called foreigners to her colours. As long ago as the reign of Louis XI in the fifteenth century, there had been a 'Scots Guard', as readers of Sir Walter Scott's *Quentin Durward* will recall. Later kings, from François I to Louis XVI, had made use of the services of Germans and Swiss. During the French Revolution, the National Assembly, faced with Prussian invasion, had created on 7 June 1792 a 'Foreign Volunteer Legion'. Several other 'legions' of Dutch, Italian and Polish troops had been raised during the Revolutionary Wars; and Napoleon had numbered among his troops the Hanoverian, Portuguese and Spanish Legions, and the Poles of the Vistula Legion. These units had fought all over Europe: at Wagram, Jena and Eylau, in Spain and in Russia.

Disbanded in 1815 following the fall of the Emperor, the remnant of these units had amalgamated and reappeared several months later under the title of 'Royal Foreign Legion'; and in 1821 this unit was retitled the 'Regiment of Hohenlohe'. Less than ten years later, in the first days of Louis-Philippe's reign, the Hohenlohe Regiment had been dis-

Polish lancer in the service of France under the First Empire (1804–15).

banded during his reorganization of the army – only to be largely reconstituted under what would become its definitive title: the Légion Etrangère or Foreign Legion.

THE OLD LEGION

Recruitment was brisk during the first six months. By September 1831, five battalions had been sent overseas, under the command of Colonel Stoffel, a Swiss officer who had served France for nearly thirty years and who fought in the ranks of Napoleon's army in Spain. These first battalions disembarked at Algiers, Oran and Bône. Their uniform was that of the line infantry of metropolitan France: crimson trousers, a royal-blue tailcoat, a heavy black shako, and an iron-grey greatcoat carried rolled in a ticking cover on the knapsack. The only distinctive sign of the Legion was the motif on the buttons, which bore the unit title encircling a five-pointed star.

While two other battalions (the Belgian 6th and the Polish 7th) were being formed in France, the Legionnaires in Algeria were serving their apprenticeship in guerrilla warfare. The style of the fighting was dictated by the enemy, in a terrain which favoured ambushes and sudden raids, followed by swift retreats. It was not until 27 April 1832 that the 1st and 3rd Battalions (composed of Swiss and Germans) recorded their first victory; on that day, they stormed the redoubts covering the approaches to Maison Carrée, a large village some miles east of Algiers. This exploit won for the Legion its first regimental colour, brought out by the new commanding officer, Colonel Combe, and bearing on its folds the inscription 'The King of the French, to the Foreign Legion'.

In October 1832, after receiving its last two battalions, the Legion boasted an effective strength of 5538 officers, NCOs and men.

ALGERIA

It was at this period that the smouldering resistance of the Arabs burst into flame, fanned by the courageous young Emir of Mascara, Abd-el-Kader. On 11 November 1832, he arrived before the gates of Oran at the head of some three thousand cavalry.

Battle was quickly joined. The first charge by the Arab horsemen was broken up on the slopes of the Djebel Tafaraouïni, a feature dominated by the little Arab shrine, or *marabout*, named Sidi Chabel. Then the French mounted a counter-attack: on the right were the Chasseurs, and on the left the Legionnaires of the 4th Battalion. This unit was composed of Spaniards, many of them guerrilla veterans of the Peninsular War against Napoleon's occupying army. They were uncouth soldiers, but crafty. They knew how to slip under a horse's belly and up on the rider's blind side, tipping him out of the saddle to be stabbed to death. Disorganized, the Arab squadrons began to break up. At nightfall, Abd-el-Kader withdrew. Oran was saved.

Soldier of the Hohenlohe Regiment (1815–30).

The following year, side by side with the Italians of the 5th Battalion, the Spaniards were at their work again. In June they took Arzew; and in July they fought in the capture, and later the defence, of Mostaganem.

On 9 April 1833, a new colonel was appointed to command the Legion. His name was Bernelle. He wrote a new victory into the record of his corps with the capture of Kolea, southwest of Algiers. But the name of Bernelle is associated, above all, with one of the cruellest ordeals that the Legion ever faced, and one which nearly destroyed it: the Spanish Carlist War of 1835–38.

SPAIN

The trouble had started in 1833, when the dying King Ferdinand VII had willed the throne to his three-year-old daughter Isabella under the regency of her mother, Queen Maria Cristina. The dead king's brother, Don Carlos, contested the child's right of succession, and led a savage insurrection in the north of the country. Under the terms of a tripartite agreement, Portugal, Britain and France decided, in June 1834, to intervene on behalf of the child queen.

The first troops to arrive were twelve thousand British, who settled down around San Sebastian. The French expeditionary force arrived rather later. It was, in fact, the Foreign Legion – signed over to Maria Cristina, in return for a promise that the troops would be supplied and paid by Spain.

At the last moment, two of its battalions – the Italian 5th and Polish 7th – were sent urgently to the assistance of a French column under attack by Abd-el-Kader's warriors near Oran. Once again, the Legionnaires performed marvels: sacrificing themselves in the rearguard, they bought time for General Trezel and his battalions to extricate themselves from a potential massacre on the Macta salt-marshes on 27–29 June 1835. No sooner had Trezel's column limped home than the Legion, reunited, was marched down to its ships. On 19 August 1835, the Foreign Legion disembarked at Tarragona.

Civil Wars are seldom chivalrous – in Spain, even less than elsewhere. Napoleon had discovered this twenty-five years before, and the world would be reminded of it again a century later. The struggle between the 'Carlists' and the queen regent's 'Cristinos' was no exception, as the Legion was to learn during the latter part of 1835 and the winter which followed. God help the man who fell into the hands of the enemy alive . . . .

In mid-September, an outpost defended by thirty Legionnaires under Sous-lieutenant Dumoustier was captured by the Carlists. It was suggested to the Legionnaires that they change sides. They refused. For several days thereafter they were dragged from village to village – bound, naked, and with their eyes put out. Eventually, they were shot. It is hardly remarkable that, when Capitaine Ferrary captured a Carlist unit, he in his turn took no prisoners.

Until April 1836, the Foreign Legion had been purely an infantry corps. Bernelle – promoted 'field marshal' by Maria Cristina – decided to convert his regiment into an autonomous command, complete with its own support and reconnaissance units. He put in hand the formation of an artillery unit, under the command of Capitaine Rousselet; a sapper unit; and several cavalry squadrons, largely composed of Polish lancers. (This was the first known attempt to form a tactically balanced 'combat group', and the last for many years to come – although it foreshadowed the methods of today's Legion.)

Another innovation, which was to prove lasting, was the mixing of nationalities, which Bernelle ordered throughout the units under his command. National quarrels, which the recruits had brought with them into the Legion and which had caused strains between different national battalions, would now become a thing of the past: with nationalities mixed within even the smallest sub-unit, they were simply impossible to sustain. Another obvious advantage was the improved coordination and unity of ideas within a regiment in which all ranks were henceforward obliged to speak French as their common language.

The year 1836 was a difficult one for the Foreign Legion. It was marked by two victorious but costly engagements: the action at Tirapegui on 24 April, and the battle of Zubiri on 1 August. At Zubiri, where the Car-

lists attacked a defensive line held by the loyalist army, the day was saved by Rousselet's guns. The Carlists fell back, but not before the Legion's 3rd and 4th Battalions had lost three hundred dead.

All Bernelle asked in return for the sufferings of his men was that the Spanish authorities keep their promise to supply him with rations, clothing and pay. It was a vain hope. The only answer he was favoured with was the suggestion that 'your men look after their greatcoats'. In the end, they were in rags. For lack of anything else, they adopted the local berets favoured by the Carlists, and replaced their ruined boots with Spanish espadrilles. Bernelle raged at the Spanish over this callous treatment – and was relieved of his command.

His successor, Colonel Conrad (christened by the Carlists 'the hero on the white horse'), would have no greater success. For two more long years, the Legion – penniless, starving and wretched – dragged itself from one battle to another, all along the foothills of the Pyrenees. Legionnaires fought in a hundred engagements; and on 2 June 1837 they came to Barbastro. It was there that Colonel Conrad was killed. It was there, too, that the 'old' Legion began its

final agony, after a murderous battle which reduced it to a single battalion. The survivors were dumped in Pamplona, where they had to endure another six months without pay or rations before their suffering came to an end.

Of nearly five thousand men who had disembarked in 1835, fewer than five hundred crossed back into France. The Spanish martyrdom was over.

THE NEW LEGION
The Legion should not have been able to survive such bloodletting; but survive it did. Even while the regiment of Bernelle and Conrad was fighting to a standstill in Spain, other foreigners were already enlisting in the south of France for service in a second Legion, destined for Algeria.

Two battalions strong, this 'new' Legion disembarked in Africa during the first days of 1837, in time to take part in the second campaign mounted by the French against the fortified city of Constantine. The previous year, a first attempt had failed to subdue this citadel, which was strongly defended, well equipped with artillery, and perched high on a rocky plateau surrounded by deep gorges. The second attempt on Constantine began in foul

The assault on Constantine. After four days of fighting, Sergent-major Doze seizes the last enemy flag on 13 October 1837.

weather on 9 October 1837, and lasted for four days. On the 13th, at the head of the storming parties, the Legion fought its way through a breach battered in the walls. All that day, they fought in the narrow streets of the old Arab town, against a bitter resistance. At last, as night fell, Sergent-major Doze of the Legion captured the last enemy flag; it is displayed today at Les Invalides in Paris.

By the beginning of 1838, the Legion fielded three battalions. Legionnaires saw action in a number of scattered engagements, notably near Algiers against the forces of Abd-el-Kader, the irreconcilable enemy. As always, they also spent much of their time in construction work. Between Douera and Boufarik they built a metalled road, which was known for many years as the 'Chaussée de la Légion' or 'Legion's Road'.

The 4th Battalion in fierce combat with Abd-el-Kader's cavalry in 1840.

THE END OF THE CONQUEST

In 1841, their numbers increasing steadily, the battalions of the Legion were regrouped into two separate regiments. The 1er Régiment Etranger (1st Foreign Regiment, abbreviated here to 1st RE) was to be based around Algiers, with its operational area in the western part of the country. It was the 1st RE which founded the town that would become the cradle of the Legion – Sidi-bel-Abbès, about sixty miles south of Oran. The regiment settled to a tireless routine of patrolling the countryside in 'flying columns': building here, fighting there, establishing outposts, laying roads, and beating off the attacks of war-parties sent out by the relentless Abd-el-Kader.

The 2nd Foreign Regiment (2nd RE) was based at Bône. From here, it turned its attention westwards, towards the Kabyle highlands, and southwards, beyond Biskra, where the sands of the Sahara lapped against the Aurès mountains. It was in the Aurès that the regiment distinguished itself on 15 March 1844, in savage fighting for one of the last strongholds of resistance in the area, the Berber village of M'Chounech. This exploit was reported to Louis-Philippe by his son, the Duc d'Aumale, who had put himself at the head of the Legionnaires. M'Chounech earned the 2nd RE a regimental colour.

The area was not pacified for long. The Chaouïa tribesmen of the Aurès were stubborn enemies, and the Saharan borders were often troubled by their forays. Apart from suppressing these enemies in the hills, the 2nd RE's Colonel Carbuccia was also ordered, in July 1849, to attack a nest of insurgents at the oasis of Zaatcha. Inadequately briefed, the colonel was surprised by the strength of the defences, and was forced to fall back after losing thirty-two dead and 115 wounded.

A second assault was soon organized, with much stronger forces: a total of four thousand men, supported by powerful artillery, under the command of General Herbillon. Even these resources were hardly overgenerous, considering the obstacles. The oasis of Zaatcha was a huge palmgrove surrounded by a ditch more than twenty feet wide, and the few routes into it were guarded by solid buildings held by experienced and determined warriors. The attack was mounted in harsh winter weather; the troops were already weakened by the cholera which had been brought into the camp by reinforcements newly arrived from France. After six weeks of grim fighting, the Legionnaires finally took Zaatcha, at bayonet-point, on 26 November 1849. Herbillon's column had suffered fifteen hundred dead and wounded.

For a period of eight years, the two regiments of the Legion marched back and forth across the length and breadth of Algeria. They built forts, cleared and marked tracks, and set up the safe markets which helped to reconcile the tribes to a more peaceful way of life. Often enough, they had to lay aside the pick and shovel and take up their rifles: although most of Algeria was more or less peaceful, there still remained scattered areas which had never submitted. This was particularly true of Kabylia. These rugged mountains, snow-covered in winter, had been notorious as a centre of fierce resistance to foreign rule, even in the days of the Pax Romana. The Romans had been forced simply to surround Kabylia and leave it to its own devices, without trying to penetrate it. Even Abd-el-Kader himself had been driven out by the independent mountain clans.

For the French, Kabylia was recognized as a potential threat to the security of their whole system in Algeria. Since 1838, many vain attempts had been made to reduce this natural fortress. In the autumn of 1856, a major offensive was mounted, and several French columns slowly converged towards the rocky heart of Kabylia. One by one, in hard fighting, the ridges and valleys were cleared; but fighting was still going on eight months later when, on 24 June 1857, the Legion added the name of Ischeriden to its battle honours.

ISCHERIDEN

Between four and five thousand Kabyle warriors were holding the crest of a steep ridge. The first French assault failed, despite artillery support. General MacMahon, commanding the column, ordered the 2nd RE into the attack. The men advanced up the slope as if on parade, in impeccable order and with shouldered arms; they did not fire a single shot. This extraordinary display of confidence disconcerted the Kabyles; and when the Legionnaires had climbed steadily up to the crest through a hail of fire, and put in their final assault with the bayonet, the tribesmen soon abandoned their position and melted away. It was only a matter of days before Kabyle resistance finally crumbled. Marshal Randon promised each village headman that the laws and customs of the tribes would be respected. He kept his word; and so did his successors.

With the battle of Ischeriden, the pacification of Algeria was effectively completed. The Legionnaires could return 'home' to Sidi-bel-Abbès.

While French troops had been fighting in Africa, France herself had undergone yet another change of regime. Swept away by the revolution of 1848, King Louis-Philippe had been replaced by the Second Republic. This new republic had hardly seen the light of day before it was strangled, on 2 December 1851, by its own president, who soon afterwards had himself proclaimed Emperor of the French with the title Napoleon III. 'The Empire means Peace', declared the new sovereign, sensitive to the fears of those who remembered uneasily the career of his late uncle, Napoleon I. For twenty years he kept his word, in the sense that he undertook no major adventures in central Europe. Even so, during this period France was constantly involved in 'limited' wars abroad. The Legion played a major part in these campaigns: in the Crimea, in Italy and in Mexico, Legionnaires were to cover themselves with glory.

SEBASTOPOL

In 1853, Tsar Nicholas I decided to seize Constantinople. His aims were to secure Russian control of the Bosphorus and free access from the Black Sea to the Mediterranean, and to give the final *coup de grâce* to the Ottoman Empire – 'the sick man of Europe'. Turkey immediately appealed to France and Britain for support, which was quickly promised. On 14 September 1854, the allies landed in the Crimea without interference. After a first victory over the Russians at the Alma, they settled down to besiege Sebastopol. It was in this fortress town, which was formidably defended for its day, that the Russian army and fleet had concentrated for the attempt on Constantinople.

The siege would last for a whole year, in appalling conditions. The horrors of the climate were aggravated by a cholera epidemic, which carried off, along with thousands of their men, the commanders of both allied expeditionary forces: Raglan and Saint-Arnaud.

Represented from the start by the 1st RE, the Legion was soon brought up to brigade strength by the arrival of reinforcements from the 2nd RE. They distinguished themselves at the Alma, and were almost alone in their pursuit of Menshikov's fleeing troops. They then took their place in the siege lines before Sebastopol. On 1 May 1855, after the armies had passed a hideous winter in the trenches, the allied command decided to mount an offensive to 'enliven' the front. It failed, at the cost of a pointless massacre. Among the Legion's 118 dead and 480 wounded fell Colonel Viénot of the 1st RE. His name lives on, commemorated in the title of the Legion's barracks, first at Sidi-bel-Abbès and subsequently at Aubagne.

On 18 June, another attack was launched, this time upon the key to the Russian position, the Malakoff redoubt. Once more, the attackers were repulsed: six thousand French and British soldiers were sacrificed in a bungled operation. On 8 September, the allies tried yet again. For once, the Legion was represented by only a handful of men; but these hundred volunteers were the spearhead of the assault, right out in front of the attack columns, carrying scaling ladders and wooden beams. By the time the main assault units reached their objectives, Sergent Valliez's Legionnaires had already built scaffolding and ramps for them against the Russian defences. That evening, the Malakoff fell at last. That same night, the Russians began to evacuate Sebastopol.

The Crimean War ended in August 1856. The reward for the Legion in the East was disbandment. The men were shipped back to Sidi-bel-Abbès, where they reenlisted in one of two new 'Legions'. For reasons too complex to explore here, it had been decided to form these two new and separate units, which kept the title of 'Legions' only between January 1855 and April 1856. In that

The 2nd Foreign Regiment advancing on Ischeriden, 24 June 1857.

month, the new '2nd Foreign Legion' (2nd LE), composed entirely of Swiss, was redesignated '1st Foreign Regiment' (1st RE); the veterans of Kabylia and the Crimea had to take a subordinate place in the line as the new '2nd Foreign Regiment'. This 2nd RE retained more or less the uniform of the line infantry: crimson trousers and blue tunics. For the time being, the Swiss 1st RE was distinguished by a green tunic. (Red and green would become, from now on, the Legion's distinctive colours, surviving in certain uniform embellishments, even when the green tunic of the short-lived 1st RE disappeared.)

It was in these uniforms that the two regiments fought against the Austrians in Italy in 1859.

MAGENTA

The French intervention in Italy was a natural consequence of Napoleon III's liberal political ideals. He had always had a great sympathy for the Italian *carbonari* – the patriots who had fought in the shadows for so long, in pursuit of the old dream of unifying their country, which at that date was still largely occupied by Austria. The campaign opened in the spring of 1859; and the Legion was there. This, its second intervention in a European war, would be brief but brilliant.

On 4 June, the town of Magenta came into sight; and so did the Austrian army. It was about 3 p.m. when the Legionnaires found themselves in thickly cultivated country, broken up by hedges and vineyards. Murderous for cavalry, it was the infantryman's natural ground. Pausing to fire volleys, the white-coated Austrians advanced among the thickets and lanes. On the left of the French line, the horsemen of the Mounted Chasseurs began to fall back.

Standing upright in his stirrups, the Legion's Colonel de Chabrière roared: 'Packs off! Forward, the Legion!' Bayonets held low, the Legionnaires charged into the attack. The momentum of this *furia francese* rocked the Austrians. They recoiled, fell back, and finally they fled. By evening, the victory was won. The next day, 5 June, Milan was liberated.

The Legion marched into the city at the head of the French army. It had earned this right by the spilling of

Death of Colonel de Chabrière at the Battle of Magenta, 4 June 1859.

its blood: fifteen Legion officers were wounded or dead, among the latter Colonel de Chabrière, and nearly three hundred NCOs and men alongside them. Three weeks later, on 24 June, the battle of Solferino brought the campaign to a close.

After a detour which brought it to Paris for its first, and triumphal, parade through the capital, the Legion returned to Algeria. It was not to remain there for long.

In October 1859, for lack of recruits, the exclusively Swiss establishment (and the green uniforms) of the 1st RE were abandoned. In December 1861, all Legionnaires were gathered once more into a single Foreign Regiment, clad in traditional blue and red.

Legion drummer in Italy, 1859.

CAMERONE

Three years after the Italian campaign, a new arena beckoned; and it was there, in Mexico, that the Legion would enter into legend.

The French expeditionary force was first sent to Mexico to protect French interests from the threat of the expansionist policies of the United States, at a time when several European nations were embroiled in the chaotic affairs of the region. The French stayed on, alone, to support the Emperor Maximilian, the puppet ruler installed by Napoleon III. The Legion was not at first included in the list of units assigned to the expeditionary force. It was a petition, sent personally to Napoleon by the young officers of the regiment, which set them on their way. Two battalions strong, the RE marched on to the transports on 9 February 1863. On 28 March, they landed at Vera Cruz.

A cruel disillusion awaited them there. The regiment had expected to march inland to Puebla, the major Juarist centre, which the French had placed under siege. Instead, the Legionnaires were given the thankless duty of providing road security along the route which led from the port up to Puebla. The Legion was stationed in the most inhospitable region of the country: the low-lying coastal 'hot lands', where cholera and yellow fever raged unchecked.

Mexico was a grim country, and Juarez's partisans gave no quarter to their enemies. The Legion was to discover this quickly. On 1 April, after a rail journey of a few miles up to the Tejera, the Legionnaires marched inland as far as Chiquihuite, where their Colonel Jeanningros established his headquarters. From place to place along the march, small detachments were left, to guard sections of the dirt road and the isolated work-camps along the planned route of the railway. On 18 April, one of these camps was attacked by the guerrilla band of Antonio Diaz, mayor of Jalapa. The place was sacked, the workers were driven off, and their escort was massacred.

Two days later, Diaz mounted another raid – but this time his intended prey was a company of the Legion. The Legionnaires counterattacked, and cut the guerrillas to pieces. The Prussian Lieutenant Milson killed Diaz with his own hand. Henceforward, the Juarists knew that the Legion was not to be trifled with.

On 29 April, just a month after the disembarkation, Colonel Jeanningros was informed that an important road convoy was leaving Vera Cruz for Puebla. Apart from three million francs in gold, rations and ammunition, the convoy included essential siege equipment whose arrival was vital to the outcome of the siege of Puebla, which had now been dragging on for a year. All too aware of the lack of security in the Legion's sector of responsibility, Colonel Jeanningros decided to send a company of Legionnaires down towards the coast to meet the convoy on its way.

The 3rd Company was available, but all its officers were laid low by sickness. Capitaine Danjou, one of the colonel's headquarters staff, volunteered to take command. Two junior headquarters officers stepped forward to fill the other gaps in the company's command: Sous-lieutenant Maudet, the colour-bearer, and Sous-lieutenant Vilain, the paymaster. Although assigned to staff duties at that time, all three were experienced combat officers.

The 3rd Company, ravaged by fever, could only put sixty-two NCOs and men on parade. Too bad. In the cool darkness an hour after midnight, the company swung off down the track. At about 2 a.m. on 30 April, they took their brief regulation rest at

The final moments of the Battle of Camerone, 30 April 1863.

Capitaine Danjou, killed at Camerone at the age of 35.

a spot called Paso del Macho, garrisoned by their comrades of Capitaine Saussier's company. They did not stay long; and 5 a.m. found them marching past the ruins of a little abandoned hamlet named Camerone.

Danjou's mission was to march to Palo Verde, where he was to search the surrounding scrub country for any Juarist ambush which might be lying in wait for the convoy. In theory, the convoy's departure from Vera Cruz was a military secret, but Danjou was too old a soldier to imagine that the enemy had not got wind of it. He was not mistaken. Ever since their departure from Paso del Macho, Danjou's company had been trailed at a distance by six hundred Juarist cavalry, led by Colonel Francisco de Paula-Milan. Warned of the convoy's departure, the Mexicans were assembling for the attack some eight hundred mounted troops, as well as the three regular infantry battalions of Jalapa, Vera Cruz and Cordoba – perhaps two thousand men in all.

As the sun climbed from the horizon, Danjou and his company left the mud-brick ruins of Camerone behind them and continued down the track towards Palo Verde. There they halted, posted sentries, and settled down to make their morning coffee. They never tasted it. Almost at once, the sentries gave the alarm: they had spotted the advance guard of the Cotaxla cavalry of Don Hilario Psario, who had been dogging their tracks since the middle of the night.

Capitaine Danjou reacted fast – so fast that his men did not have time even to refill their canteens with the water that they had poured out to make the coffee. If his Legionnaires were going to be attacked, Danjou knew that they had no chance of survival in this flat scrubland. They needed walls around them, and even the ruined walls of Camerone would afford a degree of protection. He decided to fall back towards them. In column of sections, the 3rd Company started back up the track.

It was a sensible reaction to the circumstances; but the Mexican Colonel Milan, watching from a distance, drew his own conclusions. That sudden retreat might mean that the French soldiers had spotted evidence

of the ambush which he was carefully preparing for the convoy. From that moment, the fate of the 3rd Company was sealed: it would have to be wiped out. There must be no witnesses. And if it was to be destroyed, it was vital to attack before it could reach the shelter of Camerone.

The horsemen charged straight into the attack. Danjou countered by forming square – the classic defence against cavalry. At sixty paces, the Legionnaires opened fire. The Mexican charge was broken. Using the few moments they had bought, the Legionnaires stumbled on towards the ruins. A second charge hit them when they had already reached cover. They formed square once more, fired a volley, and then counter-attacked with the bayonet, to cries of 'Vive l'Empereur!' Disengaging, they threw themselves into the shelter of a large walled yard, whose southern side lay along the Puebla road.

Only the building on the north side of the enclosure merited the name of house: a two-storey structure roofed with red tiles. The wall around the yard was ten feet high, stoutly built of stones in mud cement. On the east side of the yard, it was pierced by two open gateways; against the wall between them was a tumbledown lean-to shed. Along the inside of the long south wall was another outbuilding in slightly better condition. It was here that some of the Legionnaires took up their position. They improved it as best they could, making loopholes for their rifles.

Original decorations of Capitaine Danjou.

Opposite them, in the building on the north side, Danjou and the rest of the 3rd Company did the same. They barricaded the gateways, blocked a hole in the corner of the wall, and devised makeshift battlements.

Meanwhile, outside the walls, Colonel Milan was calling up his infantry. Marching at the double, they were drawing nearer to the wretched hamlet, where a total of eight hundred Mexican cavalrymen now only waited for the order to annihilate these sixty-five Frenchmen sheltering in the outbuildings of La Trinidad.

Milan sent forward an emissary, Lieutenant Ramon Lainé, to offer the French the chance of honourable surrender. From the roof, Sergent Morzycki, a Pole, passed on the offer to his capitaine – and translated his reply: 'Out of the question . . .'.

The assaults began almost at once. The first was launched by the dismounted Mexican cavalry, who had first stripped off their outsize spurs. The attack was driven off, but Capitaine Danjou was mortally wounded. Shortly before he died, he made his men vow that they would not surrender, but would fight to the death if they must. The Legionnaires gave him their word.

By 11 a.m., the 3rd Company had been defending their makeshift fort for three hours. They had no food; no ammunition, beyond what they carried in their pouches (the mules with the spare cartridges had stampeded during the running fight back to Camerone); and, above all, no water. The single bottle of wine had long since been shared out, a few drops for each man.

It was at this point that the three battalions of Mexican infantry came panting up. Before sending them into the attack, Colonel Milan once again offered the French the chance to surrender. The answer he received was the single short but expressive word, 'Merde!', more usually identified with General Cambronne on the battlefield of Waterloo.

The plight of the defenders was becoming desperate. Some of the Mexicans succeeded in clambering up into the top floor of the house. From this vantage point, they loosed a hail of bullets down on to the Legionnaires, and set fire to the building before abandoning it. It was at this point that Sous-lieutenant Vilain was killed.

By 5 p.m., just twelve Legionnaires remained on their feet around Sous-lieutenant Maudet. But still they held on; still the Mexicans failed to overrun their position. At one point, an eerie silence fell. The Mexicans ceased firing; and from their loopholes the French could hear Milan haranguing his men, calling down shame upon them that two thousand attackers had not yet managed to silence such a pitiful handful of defenders. Then, with drums beating and trumpets blaring, a mass of Mexicans charged into the corpse-strewn yard.

It came to hand-to-hand fighting almost at once. In a corner of the enclosure, his back to the outbuildings, Sous-lieutenant Maudet was still fighting. Nobody stood with him now but Caporal Maine, and Légionnaires Catteau, Constantin and Wenzel. At their officer's word of command, the four men fired their last cartridges; then, bayonets levelled, they moved not back, but forwards. Five men charging two thousand. Maudet took only two steps before he fell, hit by two bullets – this in spite of the devotion of Catteau, who threw himself in front of his officer, and was struck nineteen times.

Maine, Wenzel and Constantin stood alone, facing the enemy – and certain death. They were only saved by the arrival of the Mexican Colonel Combas, who forced up the rifles that were trained on the Legionnaires and called on them, for the last time, to surrender. Maine replied that they would only do so if they could keep their weapons, and if Combas would promise that their wounded would be cared for. The bayonets surrounding them trembled with menace. 'I can refuse nothing to men like you', replied Combas; and he escorted them to the astonished Colonel Milan. 'This is all there are left?', Milan exclaimed. 'Then these are not men, but demons!'

Capitaine Danjou's men had kept their word to the end. By their bitter resistance, they had forced Milan's troops, first to reveal themselves, and then to become tied down in a day-long battle. The 3rd Company of the Foreign Regiment had saved the convoy. Their sacrifice had made possible a French victory at Puebla.

Left: *A Foreign Regiment sergent and his wife (probably originally a canteen-woman) in Mexico, 1863–67.* Below: *Mme Joséphine Bossut, a canteen-woman in Mexico at the same period.*

At the request of Colonel Jeanningros, the Emperor Napoleon III decreed that the name of Camerone should be inscribed on the regimental colour. It is borne to this day on all the regimental colours and standards of the Foreign Legion. In 1892, a monument was raised on the site of the battle; and its dignified Latin inscription sums up admirably not only the final action of the 3rd Company, but also the essential spirit of the Legionnaire:

'Here stood fewer than sixty men against an entire army. Its weight overwhelmed them. Life, sooner than courage, forsook these soldiers of France.'

Each year, in every unit of the Foreign Legion, the anniversary of the battle of Camerone is celebrated with pomp and a sense of rededication. At Aubagne, the wooden false hand of Capitaine Danjou, recovered from the battlefield, is paraded before the troops as a sacred relic.

MEXICO

The Mexican campaign was not over for the Legion after the single battle of Camerone. Legionnaires continued to serve there for four more years, and distinguished themselves in a number of engagements up and down the country. This remained true, even when it had become clear that final victory would be impossible. After 1865, the United States government, free now of its preoccupation with the Civil War, took the closest interest in Mexican affairs. The Re-

public found intolerable the idea of an Emperor – a European Emperor, at that – ruling its southern neighbour by means of European bayonets. The Americans encouraged and supported Juarez and his Liberal forces against the Conservatives and Indians, who represented whatever support Maximilian could claim to enjoy among Mexicans. Little understood in France, and unpopular in America, the now pointless war became bogged down.

In Europe, there were more immediate preoccupations. At Sadowa, in 1866, a Prussian army, equipped with breech-loading rifles and rail transport, had shattered the Austrians in the climax of a war which had lasted only seven weeks. The reverberations of that thunderclap were heard all over Europe; and France's eyes turned towards her eastern frontiers. Napoleon III made up his mind to cut his losses, and brought the Mexican campaign to an end. In March 1867, the Foreign Legion returned to Algeria, leaving behind in Mexican graves thirty-one officers and 1971 NCOs and men, of whom twenty-two officers and 446 other ranks had been killed in action. What they had won for the Legion was intangible, but important.

The Legion had once been a

The Foreign Regiment before Oajacca, Mexico, in 1865.

little-respected unit, hardly better than a labour corps. Now it had a glow about it; and Camerone had given it a symbol of identity. The Legion had won the right to survive, and its continued existence would not be seriously contested again. This was doubly assured by the imminent fall of the Empire and the birth of the Third Republic, ushering in an age of great colonial expansion, in which the Legion would figure prominently.

Before that door could open, however, the Legion had a part to play on its very own soil. During the disastrous ordeal of the Franco-Prussian War, Legionnaires would participate for the first, but not the last, time in the defence of France herself.

1870–1871

At the outbreak of the Franco-Prussian War, many foreigners living in France enlisted to fight for their adopted homeland. These enthusiastic volunteers were formed into the 5th Foreign Battalion, nominally part of the Legion. They were practically wiped out before Orleans on 10 October 1870; Commandant Arago and five other officers were killed, but it is intriguing to note that among the survivors was one 'Sous-lieutenant Kara' – in fact, Prince Karageorgevich,

the future King Peter I of Serbia.

The remnant of the 5th Battalion was soon joined by two battalions formed for the campaign by the Legion in Algeria. The Legionnaires fought through a bitterly hard winter; and on 13 January they recaptured Montbéliard. But the game was already lost, and the armistice which France was forced to sign on 28 January found the Legion before Be-

Contemporary print of the Battle of Coulmiers, 9 November 1870.

sançon. On 17 March, they arrived at Versailles, having lost fourteen officers and 916 NCOs and men in action. In June 1871, the survivors of this wretched campaign returned to Algeria. At the railway station in Sidi-bel-Abbès, they were greeted by the Legion's band. The German Legionnaires left behind in Africa had guarded the Legion's traditions faithfully.

With Alsace and Lorraine lost beyond any immediate hope of recovery, the governments of the Third Republic turned their attention away from Europe and towards the unexplored vastnesses of Africa and Asia, where they hoped to establish colonies. The 19th Army Corps, the 'Army of Africa', seemed the best fitted for this mission. It was rich in fighting experience, gained over decades of active service in a harsh terrain and among a poor and disease-ridden population. For campaigns in which France would be obliged to build roads, open markets, lay out townships and sink harbours, it was natural that the Foreign Legion should figure among the units selected.

TONKIN

In 1883, the Legion was sent to Tonkin, then the northern province of the Empire of Annam, ruled from the imperial capital of Hue. Tonkin had been acknowledged as a French protectorate by the Emperor; but in practice it was a land overrun and ravaged by large bands of pirates (known as 'Black Flags'), supported by Chinese regulars sent over the border by the hostile Chinese Empress. On 8 November 1883, the 1st Battalion of the Legion disembarked at Haiphong. It was the opening scene of an epic that would last for seventy years; and for those who played a part in it, from the 1880s right up to 1954, it was unquestionably a story of love as much as one of war.

(It is one of history's paradoxes that the Legion was first sent to Tonkin to protect the Annamese population against Chinese and Thai brigands led by one Deo Van Tri. In 1953, Legion paratroopers jumped into Dien Bien Phu to protect the subjects of Deo Van Long, grandson of Deo Van Tri, against Annamese communists.)

In 1883, the commander of the expedition, Admiral Courbet, decided that he was going to clean up Tonkin. The first step would be to attack the main strongholds of the Black Flags, the forts of Son Tay and Bac Ninh. The Legion's 1st Battalion distinguished itself at the capture of Son Tay, which was defended by some twenty-five thousand of the enemy. The following year, now reinforced by the arrival of a second battalion under Commandant Hutin, the Legion took part in the storming of the citadel of Bac Ninh. Its conduct under fire prompted the commander of the operation, General de Négrier, to declare that 'the honour of being the first into Bac Ninh belongs to the Legion'. But it was to be at another old Chinese fort, named Tuyen Quang, that the Legion would show its true mettle.

Under the command of the courageous Commandant Dominé, the 1st and 2nd Companies of the 1st RE formed the backbone of a six-hundred-strong garrison which defended Tuyen Quang from 23 January until 3 March 1885. For nearly six weeks, the fort was cut off and under constant attack by an army of some twenty thousand Chinese regular troops – brave, well armed, and trained in the arts of sapping and mining.

First, the Chinese besiegers surrounded Tuyen Quang with a belt of trenches, anchored on a number of

Legionnaires of the 2nd Foreign Regiment in Tonkin, 1892.

fortified villages. From these lines, they then mounted their assaults. On 26 January, they bombarded the fort, and started fires. They then sent three columns of infantry into the assault, their objective being an exposed external blockhouse defended by men under Sergent Leber. The attackers were driven back on all sides; but by 30 January, the blockhouse, too isolated for effective support, had to be abandoned.

Events now began to move at increasing speed. The French garrison had no hope of any early help from outside, and was thrown entirely on its own resources. The Chinese kept up frequent artillery bombardments, while simultaneously driving approach-trenches towards the walls

Legionnaire in walking-out dress in Tonkin, 1890.

of the fort. Sections of the old walls collapsed. The breaches were repaired by Sergent Bobillot's sappers or by the Legionnaires, using improvised wooden palisades. The Chinese, in their turn, tried to tear these down by means of grappling-hooks thrown from their trenches. By 10 February, the Chinese sappers had reached the southeast corner of the walls; and on the 11th, they blew it up. From now on, attackers and defenders would fight face to face.

Anticipating that other breaches would inevitably be blown in the walls, Commandant Dominé ordered a second line of defences to be constructed, about sixty yards inside the old walls. With this redoubt to fall back on, the garrison continued to contest the perimeter with the Chinese. On 17 February, Capitaine Dia, commanding the garrison's company of local troops, was killed. The following day, it was the turn of Sergent Bobillot of the sappers. Four days after that, a section of the perimeter wall was blown up, and the enemy poured inside. The Legion counterattacked, despite the explosion of a sap under their very boots: twelve men were killed, but the assault was repulsed. On 24 February, almost the whole available strength of the Chinese was committed to a frenzied assault under cover of a pitch-black night. Capitaines Cattelin and Borelli led their Legionnaires in counter-attacks signalled by trumpet. Dawn saw the enemy driven out once again.

On 25 February, another mine blew up. On the 28th, more than two hundred pounds of explosive sent the last intact section of the ramparts two hundred feet into the air. For four hours, Frenchmen and Chinese fought desperately amid the ruins. But this was the final effort by the attackers. The relief column, led by General Giovaninelli, was approaching; and on 3 March, in front of their battered citadel, the survivors of the garrison presented arms to their rescuers. (This gesture would become a tradition in Indo-China.) The two Legion companies had lost a third of their strength: thirty-two dead, including one capitaine, and 126 wounded, including all the other six officers of the detachment.

At almost the same moment, another battle was taking place farther to the north, at a town which history would later make famous: Lang Son. This was one of the last actions between the French and the Chinese, and on 1 April a treaty brought the campaign to a close.

In the years that followed, the French forces devoted themselves to the slow task of pacifying a country troubled throughout its history by brigands of all kinds, and fragmented between tribes – Thais, Nungs, Meos, Mans and the rest – who nursed bitter interracial hatreds.

Here, again, the Legion played its part in the endless, patient round of building, organizing and policing, which allowed the gradual emergence of a peaceful society. It is a fact that, from about 1897 onwards, a posting to Indo-China was regarded as a holiday in a tropical paradise.

In 1930, the various units of the Legion serving in Indo-China were amalgamated under the title of 5th Foreign Infantry Regiment (5th REI).

DAHOMEY

In 1892, Ouidah, a little port on the coast of Dahomey, was one of several French trading posts scattered along the shores of Africa. Until that date, these establishments had been guaranteed by a treaty of friendship with the local king, Behanzin. For some years past, however, German agents had been stirring up trouble and had managed to persuade Behanzin that 'since 1870, France no longer exists'. The king had started to harass the French settlements, and was even threatening to wipe them out. His threats were given point by the fact that he was assembling an army and modern weapons: the acquisition of Mauser rifles was accompanied by the arrival of German instructors.

Threats seemed to be about to give way to action; and France decided to intervene. An expedition of four thousand men was sent south under the command of Colonel Dodds; it included an eight-hundred-strong Foreign Legion battalion, led by Commandant Faurax. Its mission: to seize the capital, Abomey, and to force Behanzin to negotiate. Disembarkation took place without incident on 26 August 1892. A few days later, Faurax's Legionnaires began their march up-country. They were supposed to link up with a detachment already sent ahead to pacify the Décamé area, along the banks of the river Ouémé.

For the first ten days, from 1 to 10 September, everything went well enough. The advance was hardly rapid: the compass needle was their only guide, and the path had to be hacked with machetes through the thorns and lianas of the virgin jungle. The Legionnaires toiled on across an unhealthy terrain, criss-crossed with marshes haunted by poisonous insects, of which the mosquito was not the worst. At last, on 11 September, Faurax reached the banks of the Ouémé and joined up with the first column. They marched on together; and on the night of 18 September, they bivouacked at Dogba, a riverside hamlet. Backed up against the river bank, the camp was entrenched on its other three sides – just in case. It proved a wise precaution.

At dawn on the 19th, just as the bugler was about to sound reveille, the thickets and underbrush all around the camp were suddenly alive with Dahomeyan warriors. Some even flung themselves down on the French from the overhanging trees. In moments, a mêlée of indescribable confusion was taking place. But as soon as the first shock was past, the Legion reacted: its traditional response to this sort of problem was an instant counter-attack with the bayonet. French shouts began to answer the warriors' war-cries. Some of those warriors were armed with new Mauser rifles and Winchester repeater carbines. Four times the Dahomeyans rushed in; four times they were driven back. Hand-to-hand fighting lasted until about 10 a.m., when the attackers suddenly turned tail and disappeared into the jungle. They left 832 of their dead on the ground. On the French side, the column had suffered forty-five dead, including Commandant Faurax of the Legion. His last words had been to

Legionnaires in Tonkin in 1925, on a reconnaissance patrol towards the Chinese border.

Colonel Dodds: 'Were you satisfied with my men?'

Two weeks later, at Poguessa on 4 October, Sous-lieutenant Amelot was killed. As the march dragged on, the enemy were always there. Flitting along the flanks of the column, they darted out to harass it whenever a chance offered. In the course of these running fights, they sent against the French a group of women warriors – redoubtable fighters, who neither expected mercy nor offered it. To the distress of the Legionnaires, they fought to the death rather than be taken prisoner.

In the last week of October, Colonel Dodds halted and rested his men. He did not reach Abomey until 17 November – by which time Behanzin had fled, leaving his capital in flames. In the stone-built cellar of his palace, the Legionnaires discovered a stock of excellent champagne, Bordeaux and vermouth: a small consolation. They took back to Sidi-bel-Abbès a royal trophy – a white parasol, its edge decorated with fifty human lower jaws. Of the eight hundred Legionnaires who had sailed south, 450 returned unscathed to Algeria.

FRENCH SUDAN

Soon after the expedition against Behanzin, the Legion was summoned to take part in another campaign against an African potentate who traded in slaves – Samory, Emir of Bissandougou. A ferocious and unscrupulous adventurer, he had carved an empire for himself in the valleys of Upper Niger and Upper Senegal.

The fight against Samory, and against his ally the Sultan Ahmadou, would last all of twenty years; but the participation of the Legion – 120 men and four officers in 1892, and a second small detachment in 1894 – would be limited. The most important Legion operations were in the region of Kayes in May 1893, and subsequently in the Timbuktu area. It was there that a *sous-officier* named Sergent Minnaërt, who had already earned a considerable reputation at the taking of Son Tay ten years before, would once again cover himself with glory.

As the nineteenth century drew to its close, it was, above all, in Madagascar and in the South Oran province of Algeria that the Legion

Attacking the village of Apka, Dahomey, 14 October 1892.

would add even further to its reputation.

MADAGASCAR

'When a French soldier goes into hospital, it is to have himself sent home. With an African Tirailleur, it is to be healed. With a Legionnaire, it is to die.' To confirm the truth of this grim epigram, coined by an army medical officer, it is only necessary to consider the eloquent figures for the Madagascar campaign. Total effective strength of the expeditionary force: 21,600 men. Killed in battle: 7. Died of wounds: 13. Died from 'sundry other causes': 5736.

At the climax of a quarrel between the French Republic and Madagascar's Queen Ranavolo, who refused to honour a treaty of 1885, Paris decided to send an expeditionary force: after Dahomey, it was now the turn of the 'Great Island' to feel the weight of French arguments. The defeat of 1870 was long past; besides, that had been the defeat of the Empire – the Republic was vigorous, twenty-three years old, liberal and well-intentioned.

Disembarking at Majunga on 23 April 1895, a battalion of the Legion (which formed, with two battalions of Tirailleurs, the 'Algerian Regiment') was given the mission of advance guard to General Duchêne's ex-

peditionary force. On 4 May, the Legion began its march; or, to be more precise, it began to build a road to march on.

The expedition's objective was Tananarive, 250 miles south in the mountains. Building the track and fighting – only stopping fighting to return to the task of road-building – the French column took three-and-a-half months to cover that distance.

'Every blow of the pick brings on another attack of fever', noted Capitaine Roulet of the 2nd Brigade. 'The men fall like flies. It is pitiful to see these unfortunate soldiers, who began the campaign so full of spirits and hope, now dying without a murmur of complaint, pick in hand, of the fever or heatstroke, which carries a man off in three or four hours. Their graves mark the sites of each night's halt.'

At the end of July, after going through the motions of putting up a defence, the army of the dominant Hova tribe abandoned its strong position at Andriba, the gateway to the High Plateaux. The French road reached this point on 26 August. There were still 125 miles to go.

At this stage, it was decided to form a light column of four thousand of the fittest men, who would push ahead in a forced march on Tananarive. Once again, the Legion was at the front. Departing on 14 September, the column arrived before the Malagasy capital on the 26th. The Hova army, which had sworn to die rather than surrender, dissolved without a fight.

The next day, General Duchêne addressed the Legionnaires: 'It is thanks to you, gentlemen, that we are here at all. If ever I have the honour to command another expedition, I shall ask for at least a battalion of the Foreign Legion.' Seven months later, when General Galliéni was appointed governor-general of Madagascar, he expanded on this flattering proposal: 'I want six hundred Legionnaires, so that, should the occasion arise, I can die decently.' His request was answered in fuller measure than he had hoped: until 1905 there would be an entire regiment of the Legion stationed in Madagascar.

SOUTH ORAN

The nineteenth century came to an end. In its far-flung outposts, the Legion worked on. Legionnaires constructed forts, opened roads, built schools and marketplaces. In Algeria, the Legion made a contribution to the building of a viable nation, playing a part in the whole programme of public works: agriculture, roads and railways, bridges, mines, quarries – even archaeology.

Sidi-bel-Abbès, the cradle of the Legion, had grown in sixty years from six thousand to forty thousand inhabitants. It was a model modern town, designed and entirely built by the Legion. Sidi-bel-Abbès became more than just a symbol of what the Legion could do: it was almost a religion. The men did almost everything that had to be done with their hands, a pick, a shovel and – as a proud inscription would soon declare – with their indomitable will. They were masons, navvies, plumbers, landscapers, gardeners; in time, they would become electricians, bulldozer drivers, and mechanics. At one time, town councillors would even be elected from the ranks of these foreign soldiers – surely a unique event in the history of participatory democracy.

Although Algeria was modernizing herself, the security of her frontiers was still threatened. This was particularly true in the wastes of South Oran province, where the border with Morocco to the west was

Head of a Legionnaire serving in Madagascar in 1895.

fluid, imprecise and the scene of constant conflict.

For ten years, pillaging tribes from the south had caused a growing security problem, confident that they could continue to enjoy effective immunity. In theory, the Sultan of Morocco was the sovereign of these nomadic tribes. In practice, he was almost powerless: each petty chief was the lord of a territory which he could enlarge, or exchange for another, at his own pleasure. It was for this reason that the French military command – in the person of the great Lyautey – soon felt obliged to extend French authority into Morocco, nominally in order to enforce the rule of the distant Sultan. The history of this intervention is inseparable from the history of the Foreign Legion; and, above all, from the history of those most original of units, the Compagnies Montées or Mounted Companies.

Nothing could bear less resemblance to the proud *méharistes* on their swift camels, or the brilliant red-cloaked horsemen of the Spahis, than these Mounted Companies of the Foreign Legion. These were not parade troops. Their purpose was simply to march – far and fast. They looked like a bunch of poor rustics beside the dashing cavaliers of French North Africa. But they had a secret weapon: the two-man mule.

The mule carried the stripped-down campaign equipment of two Legionnaires; six days' rations, precisely calculated and based on *kessra*, a sort of Arab wheat biscuit, together with dried dates or figs; its own fodder; and the team's water-bottles, from which the mule, too, learned to drink. It also carried one of the two men, who took it in turns to ride.

The exploits of these Mounted Companies were achieved largely through their mobility. They could cover up to forty miles in a day's march, and sometimes even completed ninety miles in two days. This was often the key to success: their unexpected appearance among the raiders put surprise on their side. There were incessant fights against the hostile tribesmen – usually victorious, sometimes tragic.

On 30 July 1900, at Taghit, some forty-five miles from Colomb Béchar, the Mounted Company of the 2nd RE was attacked by about nine hundred Doui Menia warriors, a third of them horsemen. For five hours, Lieutenant Pauly's platoon held off repeated attacks, at the cost of six dead. Three years later, on 2 September 1903, occurred the battle of El Moungar which, in the epic of the Legion, has often been compared with Camerone itself.

Once again, it was the Mounted Company of the 2nd RE which was involved. A half-company, under the command of Capitaine Vauchez, was entrusted with escorting a convoy of six hundred baggage camels to Taghit. The escort was surprised at the defile of El Moungar by a large

Two-man mule team of a Mounted Company in Morocco in 1924.

war-party – perhaps as many as two thousand followers of the rebel chief Bou Amama. For eight long hours, the 113 other ranks and two officers held out among the rocks. Early in the battle, Lieutenant Selchauhansen, a young Danish officer who was already something of a Legion celebrity, was killed. His men died around him, protecting his body from Berber mutilation. Not far away, Capitaine Vauchez calmly watched himself dying of a chest wound, still directing the defence of his Legionnaires. They had no rations, no water, and very little ammunition. At last, at 5 p.m., a relief column arrived, and the Chaambas retired. The Mounted Company of the 2nd RE had resisted to the limits of its endurance. It had lost thirty-three dead, including both officers, and forty wounded.

It was this incident that persuaded Colonel Lyautey, who had arrived from Tonkin with a brilliant reputation, to take action inside Morocco. This intervention may be said to have lasted until 1934, long after the surrender of Abd-el-Krim and the subjugation of the Taza region (described below). But in the meantime, in Europe, a greater storm was coming.

THE GREAT WAR

On 2 August 1914, the French army mobilized. The First World War was declared. Soon, like their forefathers of 1870, many foreigners living in France decided to enlist in defence of their adopted homeland. More than fifty nationalities would be represented – from Europe itself, and from Africa, Asia and America.

These volunteers were at first assembled in training camps around Paris before being, in part, leavened with Legionnaires shipped over from Algeria and Morocco. Four regiments were constituted in this way in September 1914. Two of them (the II/1st RE and the II/2nd RE) were built around officers and NCOs from the Legion's North African garrisons. The III/1st RE, formed in Paris, included drafts from the police and fire brigade. The IV/1st, entirely composed of Italians and commanded by a grandson of the great Garibaldi, would soon find itself repatriated to its country of origin, when Italy entered the war.

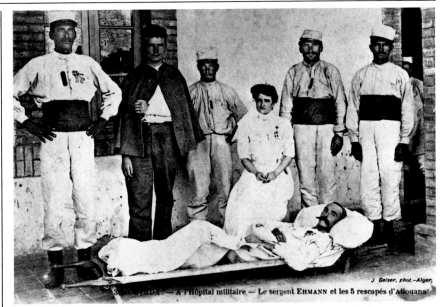

The only survivors of the Battle of Alouana, Morocco, May 1911.

Legionnaire in 1915, and (right) in Algerian uniform during the winter campaign in France, 1914–15.

In the trenches in France, 1914.

The II/1st RE had the honour of seeing action first. It was committed to the battle of Artois in May 1915, when it launched an attack on the so-called 'White Works' on Hill 140, an enemy position near Neuville-Saint-Vaast. At this stage of the war, the French infantry still wore their famous crimson trousers – a superb target for the German machine guns. By nightfall, the objective had been taken – but at such a cost that the regiment, bleeding to death, was forced to fall back without exploiting its success. From a strength of 2900, they had lost their commander, Colonel Cot; all the battalion commanders, Commandants Mullet, Gaubert and Noiré; fifty other officers; and 1889 NCOs and men.

Painfully brought up to strength once more, the II/1st RE was sent into the attack again on 16 June before Givenchy. The price of this new and equally futile attempt to break through the enemy front was twenty-one officers and 624 men dead, wounded or missing. In September 1815, the II/1st RE was again in action, at 'Navarin Farm' in Champagne, east of Berry-au-Bac. This time, the casualties were so heavy that the regiment had to be disbanded.

In the meantime, the II/2nd RE, the sister regiment, had not been spared. They had also fought in Champagne, in the Rheims and Paissy sectors; and, in September, they too had been sent into action at Souain and Navarin Farm.

The remnants of the II/1st and II/2nd RE were collected together, and combined into the Régiment de Marche de la Légion Etrangère, the Foreign Legion Marching Regiment (RMLE). Henceforward, the Legion would be represented at the front by this single regiment. But what a regiment! In exactly three years, from its formation on 11 November 1915 until the Armistice of 11 November 1918, the RMLE would make itself the most decorated regiment in the French army. The price of this honour would be a 'butcher's bill' of 139 officers, 349 *sous-officiers* and 3628 légionnaires dead or missing, to say nothing of the wounded. The epic story of the RMLE would fill volumes; here it must be limited to the barest mention of places and dates.

The young regiment's first major action took place in July 1916 at Belloy-en-Santerre, near Roye and Amiens. It lasted five days, from 4 to 9 July, and cost the regiment twenty-five officers and 844 men dead. Among them was a young American writer and poet named Alan Seeger. Shortly before his death he had written:

I have a rendezvous with Death
At some disputed barricade
When Spring comes back with rustling
* shade*
And apple-blossoms fill the air –
I have a rendezvous with Death
When Spring brings back blue days
* and fair.*

It may be he shall take my hand
And lead me into his dark land
And close my eyes and quench my
* breath –*
It may be I shall pass him still.
I have a rendezvous with Death
On some scarred slope of battered hill,
When Spring comes round again this
* year*
And the first meadow-flowers appear.

God knows 'twere better to be deep
Pillowed in silk and scented down,
Where Love throbs out in blissful sleep,
Pulse nigh to pulse, and breath to
* breath,*
Where hushed awakenings are dear
* . . .*
But I've a rendezvous with Death
At midnight in some flaming town,
When Spring trips north again this
* year,*
And I to my pledged word am true,
I shall not fail that rendezvous.

(Seeger's father went to France after the war and searched in vain for his son's grave. Finally, he bought a bell for the church in Belloy, and had it christened with his son's name. So the young poet's voice is not silenced after all: twice a day, he sings the Angelus.)

From 23 December 1916 until the beginning of April 1917, the RMLE took part in a whole series of actions, as widely scattered as they were limited. This perpetual shifting about the front earned it the nickname of '1st Removals Regiment'.

In April 1917, France's great spring offensive was unleashed. The Moroccan Division, in which the RMLE served, was to attack the enemy trenches northeast of Rheims, on the Suippe. The Legion's task was to take a position known as 'the Bay', on the edge of the village of Aubérive. On 17 April, the RMLE sprang from their jumping-off trenches.

They did not get far. The artillery preparation had been insufficient, and the German machine-gun nests were still intact. The Legionnaires improvised. They slipped forward in small groups, clearing the ground yard by yard with hand grenades. Each communication trench, each strongpoint, each shell-hole was an isolated battlefield, to be won by hand-to-hand fighting. This bloody and merciless struggle lasted four days – four days, at the end of which the RMLE had captured four-and-a-half miles of German trenches. Exhausted, the Legionnaires were pulled out of the front line. For this feat of arms, they received their fifth mention in dispatches.

A few days later, a new commander arrived to take the place left vacant by Colonel Duriez's death at Aubérive. This Lieutenant-colonel Rollet was already a famous name in the Legion. Not long before, he had served in the Mounted Companies in South Oran and Morocco. He was a small, dry man with a bristling beard, who always wore his old desert uniform – a sand-coloured tunic without a shirt, and boots without socks. Rollet soon revealed himself as the leader the regiment had been waiting for. He would lead it to glory, and in the process would earn himself the title of 'Father of the Legion'.

After a brief episode in Paris, where the President of the Republic personally pinned to the colour of the RMLE the yellow and green lanyard of the Military Medal, the regiment found itself, in August 1917, in the Verdun sector. In the general plan for the recapture of positions lost to the enemy since the previous January, the Legion's objectives were listed as the 'White Works', the eastern part of Cumières Wood, the village of Cumières, and Forges Wood. This was an extremely ambitious programme; some thought it impossible.

Anyone who thought so did not know Rollet and his regiment. They not only took their objectives; they took them well inside the time allowed. They then exploited their success by continuing the attack, taking the village of Régnaville and being the first to reach the banks of the Meuse. In comparison with the price the regiment had paid in previous battles, the Legion's losses in this operation – just fifty-three dead – were minimal. Their new colonel's economy with their lives was not lost on the Legionnaires.

At the beginning of 1918, the German spring offensive burst on the British sector of the front at Saint-Quentin. On 21 March, the allied front line gave way. On 2 April, the Legion was sent hurriedly to the Amiens sector, which was threatened by the rapid German advance. The Legionnaires dug in; and, on 25 April, they went over to the attack. Their objective was Hangard Wood. They took it, in an appalling bloodbath, during which the men of the Legion proved yet again their cold-blooded courage. Left without officers after the slaughter of the first waves of the attack, the 1st Battalion of the RMLE was commanded for a time by a private soldier – Légionnaire Kemmler, a volunteer from Luxembourg. Finally, the enemy were forced to abandon their positions and fall back. The door to Amiens was shut; and it stayed shut. The Legion's reward was a seventh mention in dispatches.

On 6 May 1918, the RMLE was once again resting in the Versigny area. It was to be a short rest, for, on 27 May, the Germans threw in a new attack which smothered the Chemin des Dames defences and reached the Marne near Château Thierry. French reinforcements were immediately diverted to this sector. On 29 May, the RMLE arrived in the vicinity of Saconin-Breuil, south of Soissons, which had fallen to the enemy. Here again, Rollet's men set an example for the rest of the army. Under a merciless hammering, the Legionnaires clung on to their positions: they knew that, if they broke, the road to Paris lay open. In his memoirs, the German General Ludendorff would recall how much the defence of Saconin had contributed to the failure of his plan.

For the Legion, as for all the allied armies, the moment was approaching when it could at last mount a decisive offensive itself. At dawn on 18 July 1918, the allies hurled themselves forward. The Legion was at Saint-Pierre-Aigle. Supported by Renault light tanks, the RMLE made rapid progress: in a few hours, it had captured two-and-a-half miles of enemy territory – a significant advance by the deathly slow standards of 1915–18. Three days later, the Legionnaires were still fighting, hurrying the German retreat on its way. Their losses were heavy – 780 officers and men, including Commandant Marseille and Capitaine de Sampigny, successive commanders of the 3rd Battalion. But they had taken 450 prisoners, and captured twenty guns.

From 2 September to 14 September, the RMLE was once again committed to battle. This time, its mission was to help break through the powerfully fortified, and until now invulnerable, Hindenburg Line. Late in August, an American attack had been repulsed; now it was the Legionnaires' turn to try. On 1 September, they took over the sector. On the 2nd, the Legion took Terny-Sorny. On the 5th, the 3rd Battalion

Above: *American volunteers in September 1915, among them Alan Seeger (third from left).* Left: *American volunteers in the 2nd RE in Paris, August 1914.*

took Sorny, Neuville-sur-Margival and the Vauxaillon Tunnel. And so it went on, for thirteen days without rest. The regiment performed miracles: Maire's 3rd Battalion alone took more prisoners than its own full strength. On 17 September, the objective was achieved. A hole had been torn in the Hindenburg Line.

During the first days of

Light infantryman of the RMLE in 1918.
Right: *Hangard Wood, April 1918.*

November, the RMLE was preparing for the great attack which was planned for the recapture of Metz. It was due to begin on 15 November, but the cease-fire of the 11th brought the war to an end. The job of the Foreign Legion Marching Regiment was done.

The RMLE had deserved well of France; and though the regiment would disappear, its spirit would not be allowed to die. The regimental colour, decorated with the Military Medal and the Legion of Honour, nine times mentioned in dispatches, was entrusted to a new regiment – the 3rd REI – which in its turn would add lustre to the Legion's laurels in the coming Moroccan campaigns.

THE EASTERN FRONT

Before closing the record of the First World War, one must mention a battalion of the Legion which fought in the French Army of the East, first against the Turks at the Dardanelles and later against the Bulgarians in Serbia. Two battles merit particular mention: the first, on 16 November

A Legion machine-gun section breaks a Turkish attack at the Dardanelles, May 1915.

1915, at the 'Saw Teeth'; and the second, after a terrible retreat, at the entry into Monastir alongside the Serbian cavalry. By that time, the Legion battalion was down to two hundred men, commanded by an adjudant-chef, all its officers having been either killed or wounded. The battalion was subsequently disbanded.

Another small unit of Legionnaires – three rifle companies with a machine-gun company in support – took part in the fierce fighting against the Bolsheviks in northern Russia, during the allied intervention in 1918–19. After fighting to help bar the Red Army's advance on Archangel, the unit – curiously – was disbanded on the spot. Many of its men promptly enlisted in the White Army, and fought in the defence of Petrograd. Some months later, a number of survivors of the battalion managed to make their way back to Sidi-bel-Abbès.

LYAUTEY AND MOROCCO
In August 1914, the attention of the French government was fully engaged in Europe. In Morocco, the resident-general, Lyautey, received terse orders: he was simply to hold on to 'Useful Morocco' – that small percentage of the country that was

pacified, inland from the coastal enclaves. Such orders took little account of Lyautey's character. He believed that to give up the initiative of operations would make ultimate retreat inevitable. Accordingly, with the weak forces left to him, he pressed on with the task which he had originally undertaken.

Among the troops still under his command were two Marching Regiments of the Legion, and two Mounted Companies. Sorely under-strength, these hard-pressed units were almost entirely composed of Germans, Austrians, Bulgarians and Turks, who could obviously not be employed in the European campaigns of 1914–18. Faithful to their motto, 'Honour and Fidelity', these Legionnaires proved their mettle by handing back to their comrades, returning from the holocaust of the Western Front, the heritage which had been entrusted to their care – intact.

Peace returned to Europe, and the Legion to North Africa. There it licked its wounds, reorganized itself, and accepted into its ranks the debris of the beaten armies, together with men of many other nations who found it hard to live without the rugged comradeship they had discovered in uniform. This flood of recruits allowed

the Legion to re-form the glorious RMLE under the new name 3rd Foreign Infantry Regiment (3rd REI). The 2nd RE, henceforward 2nd REI, left its old station at Saïda in Algeria and transferred to Morocco; and the remnants of the units which had held Morocco during the First World War were amalgamated into a new 4th REI.

These regiments, together with a new Foreign Cavalry Regiment (REC), whose formation had required the addition of the word 'Infantry' in the other regimental titles, took part in all the operations between 1920 and 1925 that led to the pacification of northern Morocco. This was a period which saw much activity by mobile columns.

In 1923, Lyautey determined to clean up the 'Tache de Taza' – the 'Taza Stain' (a region marked as a grey tint on the map of Morocco) – which was a formidable natural fortress in the mountainous Djebel Tichoukt region, and was the major refuge and base of operations for the remaining hostile tribes in that part of the country. These war-parties were large and determined. On 6 May the previous year, at Scoura, the 3rd Battalion of the 3rd REI (III/3rd REI) had won a mention in dispatches for its twelve-hour battle with Aït Tserouchen warriors, who outnumbered Chef de bataillon Nicolas's Legionnaires by two to one.

Other dangers now threatened

Marshal Lyautey's dedication to the Legion: '. . . my troop, my dearest troop.'

the northern frontier. In Spanish Morocco, a determined nationalist leader, Abd-el-Krim, incited the savage Berber tribesmen of the Rif mountains to rebellion. Soon it was more than just a revolt; it turned into a full-scale war, with 100,000 Riffs in the field, supported by artillery manned by European mercenaries. Although he had been victorious against the Spanish in 1921, and against the French in 1924 and early 1925, Abd-el-Krim was halted in the latter year and put on the defensive. All the Legion regiments in Morocco took part in this campaign; and, in May 1926, the 2nd REI fought in the decisive battles, at Djebel Iskritten and Targuist. On 26 May, Abd-el-Krim surrendered.

In that same year, a number of operations were carried out successfully in the stubborn Tache de Taza. Djebel Tichoukt, Djebel Trankrarauf, Djebel Taskert, the Tizi Tamiat – all fell one by one during the summer of 1926; and, on 14 July, a battalion of the 1st REI celebrated Bastille Day in battle on the Tizi N'Ouidel. At last, on 25 July 1926, the final hide-outs in the Taza region were cleared.

It would be another seven years, however, before Lyautey considered that his task was completed. The final campaign of pacification in southern Morocco centred on the Djebel Sagho, where the last remaining insurgents were dug in among the desolate cliffs and ridges. The Legion was prominent in the final battles; and after an encirclement of forty-two days, the last rebel chief submitted on 24 March 1933.

THE 'ROYAL FOREIGNERS'

By the time the RMLE left France for Morocco at the end of the First World War, the French high command had had plenty of opportunities to appreciate the qualities of the Legionnaires. There was serious discussion of plans to create a complete brigade of the Legion. On 5 August 1920, the French President promulgated a law, which was adopted by the Chamber of Deputies and the Senate, authorizing the creation of a foreign cavalry and a foreign artillery regiment and a battalion of foreign engineers. In the event, only the first of these units would see the light of day.

Between December 1920 and May 1921, four squadrons were successively formed at Saïda in Algeria

under the supervision of the 2nd REI. They were then sent to Tunisia, which had been chosen as the base for the new 1er Régiment Etrangère de Cavalerie – First Foreign Cavalry Regiment (1st REC). The officers and many *sous-officiers* came from French metropolitan or North African cavalry units, such as the Spahis and African Chasseurs; and some senior ranks were transferred from the Foreign Infantry Regiments. The men came, in great part, from two particular national groups: White Russians from the armies of Wrangel and Denikin, who had found their way west after defeat at the hands of the Red Army in 1920; and Germans and Hungarians, fleeing their disintegrating countries. The operational value which the 1st REC would soon demonstrate was guaranteed by the high proportion of experienced, professional cavalrymen, many of whom had been NCOs or even officers in their armies of origin.

SYRIA

In 1925, the political and military situation in Syria – which the League of Nations had placed under French mandate at the end of the First World

A Legion post in the Rif mountains, Morocco, 1925.

Lt Solomirsky of the 1st REC leading a charge at the Battle of Tizroutine, Morocco, September 1925.

Legionnaire in Morocco, 1925–30.

War – was deteriorating. For more than five years, the supporters of a plan for a 'Pan-Arabic Kingdom' had been openly stirring up anti-French feeling among the Druzes. The death of the Emir Selim, the pro-French governor of the Djebel Druze, was the spark which set off open revolt among the tribes. Soueïda was threatened by seven thousand Druze warriors. On 22 July 1925, they cut to pieces the column led by Capitaine Normand, and the surviving infantry-

men and Spahis took refuge in the old Turkish fort at Soueïda. A relief column set out, but was attacked in its turn on 2–3 August, losing nearly six hundred dead and three hundred wounded. General Sarrail, the commander-in-chief in the Levant, requested reinforcements. The 4th Squadron of the 1st REC was shipped from Tunisia with all haste, landing at Beirut on 20 August. By the 24th, they were at Damascus, ready for action.

Commanded by Capitaine Landriau, the squadron comprised five French officers and 165 NCOs and men, mainly Russians and Germans. Among them was a former Tsarist cavalry colonel and White Army general, now serving as a légionnaire, despite his snowy beard.

On 2 September, the squadron linked up with Commandant Kradzert's V/4th REI, and the two Legion units headed for an operational area in the Ezraa-Soueïda sector, some forty-five miles south of Damascus. On 11 September, they received orders to take up a defensive position at Messifré, a little market town broken up by gardens and a maze of walls. On the 16th, a patrol was attacked by eight hundred Druzes, but managed to break away at the cost of one dead and four wounded. Intelligence was received to the effect that three thousand rebels were moving on Messifré.

On 17 September, at 1 a.m., the

attack hit them. Waves of warriors on foot, followed by horsemen, hurled themselves at the entrenched positions held by the Legionnaires. The Druzes managed to reach the foot of the walls, despite a murderous fire from automatic weapons and 37 mm. guns. In continual danger of being overrun, the Legionnaires fought all night, at point-blank range and often hand-to-hand. The cavalry's horse lines were broken into, and all the guards killed. It was not until mid-morning that the attackers, failing to overcome the bloody resistance of the Legionnaires, began to falter and fall back, carrying off their dead. It was only on the second night, after a bombardment by three French aircraft, that they finally withdrew.

This check to the rebels, which cost them about five hundred dead, the same number of wounded, and eight flags, opened the road to besieged Soueïda. The fort was liberated by the Gamelin Column on 26 September. Of the French forces' forty-seven dead and eighty-three wounded at Messifré, the Legion's cavalry squadron had suffered an officer and fifteen men dead and twenty-five wounded, and had lost all its horses. The IV/1st REC was mentioned in dispatches of the Army of the Levant by General Sarrail.

After being re-formed at Rayack, the Legion cavalry unit was ordered to operate as part of a cavalry column to the west of Mount Hermon. On 5 November, the column – comprising the IV/1st REC and a squadron of the 12th Spahis – set up quarters in the old citadel of Rachaya, a half-ruined fort dominating a large village of some three thousand inhabitants. Reconnaissance indicated that about three thousand rebels were converging on the fort. Patrols were increased, and the position was put in a state of defence. On the 18th, two sections were attacked while on patrol, fighting their way out for the loss of two dead, three wounded and three missing. On the 20th, the watering party came under heavy fire from the surrounding hilltops. On the 21st, all communications were cut, and the Druzes began to infiltrate their men into the village.

The first major enemy attack, later on the 21st, carried the southern tower of the old citadel, which overlooked the rest of the position. Despite fierce resistance, its occupants were killed to a man. On the morning of the 22nd, the fighting resumed on the very ramparts of the fort. In the face of the savage resistance of the Legionnaires, who were already running short of ammunition, the enemy fell back at about 3 p.m.; but, strongly reinforced, they returned to the assault at about 5 a.m. on the 23rd. With three légionnaires, Adjudant-chef Gazeau defended the entrance to the citadel with hand grenades. A counter-attack with the bayonet briefly cleared the southern access; but, at 10 a.m., another rush by the Druzes overwhelmed the defenders of the gate. The Legionnaires fell back on the northern range of buildings.

Now under point-blank fire, the garrison held on to these positions, thanks to two more bayonet charges, but at a cost of about one hundred wounded. The position was looking desperate when French aircraft suddenly appeared, and bombed the enemy massed around the walls. A relief column was reported to be approaching; and that night the garrison was able to snatch some rest. On the following morning, 24 November, there was another enemy attack, but it was not pressed home; and at about

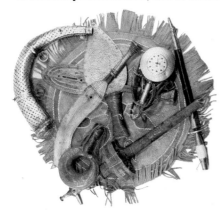

Side arms captured by the Legion in the Syrian and North African campaigns.

11 a.m., the siege was lifted. The Druzes pulled back into the mountains, having lost some four hundred dead. The Legion squadron had lost twelve dead and thirty-four wounded. Once again, it received a mention in dispatches.

In four months' campaigning, Capitaine Landriau's cavalry had proved that they had nothing to learn

from the Legion's foot-sloggers. They had justified the claim of the 1st REC to a place at the head of the Legion's columns – a claim which would be immortalized in the regimental song: 'When a Foreign Legion column marches through the Syrian *bled*, It is the 1st Foreign Cavalry that forms the column's head.'

THE APPROACH OF WAR

In 1934, after twenty-seven years of fighting and toiling, the Legion took part in the last skirmishes of the long campaign, during which it had set its seal on the pacification of Morocco. A heroic epic had drawn to a close. The regiments settled down in their garrisons, but the Legionnaires were given no opportunity for idleness. In

the old tradition of Lyautey, they worked to build a stable, modern state in Morocco. They stacked their rifles and took up their picks and shovels.

Although they were responsible for building forts, roads, bridges and railways, the most evocative symbol of their handiwork would be the famous tunnel of Foum-Zabel. Here, between 24 July 1927 and 6 March 1928, the Pioneer Company of the 3rd REI drove a tunnel through the solid rock of the hillside, 200 feet long, 25 feet wide and 10 feet high, with no tools but picks, crowbars and shovels. At the entrance to the tunnel, a simple inscription summed up their pride in this achievement: 'The mountain barred our way. The

General Rollet, 'Father of the Foreign Legion' and its first Inspector General in 1931.

order was given to pass, nonetheless. The Legion carried it out'.

It was during this period that the Foreign Legion, deeply involved in its duties from Morocco to Tonkin, from the Sahara to Mauritania, began to discover its own mystique. It was approaching its hundredth anniversary. To commemorate the centenary, Rollet, now a general and soon to be the Legion's first Inspector General, decided to erect the most splendid war memorial ever built. The work was carried out without any financial help from the government. The Legion's Monument to the Dead, raised in 1931 at Sidi-bel-Abbès, was dismantled in 1962 and brought back to Aubagne, where it stands today. It is the beating heart of the Legion; the knot that ties together all those unifying bonds of the great Foreign Legion family, across all the generations and every continent in the world.

But elsewhere, storm-clouds were gathering; and on 3 September 1939, France and her allies were at war once more. It was the beginning of six years of darkness.

THE 1940 CAMPAIGN

Just as in 1870 and 1914, foreigners resident in France enlisted in the ranks of the French army in their thousands. They were formed into three regiments: the 21st, 22nd and 23rd Marching Regiments of Foreign Volunteers (RMVE). Two more Foreign Infantry Regiments were also formed – the 11th and 12th REI – by recalling reservists to serve under officers and NCOs from the active list. The 97th Foreign Divisional Reconnaissance Group (GERD 97) was also formed, from Legion cavalry.

The 11th REI, the first of these units to be formed, was also the first under fire. On 11th June 1940, in the Verdun sector, it distinguished itself during the heroic defence of Inor Wood against a German division. It was almost completely wiped out. The survivors fought on until the armistice of 22 June, when forced at last to lay down their arms, they were disbanded and the regimental colour was burned. Of seven hundred Legionnaire prisoners, nearly five hundred escaped from Verdun. They would reappear later in North Africa, the backbone of General de Lattre's army of 1943.

Top: *The Foum-Zabel tunnel, cut by the Legion in 1928.* Above: *The Monument to the Dead being dismantled at Sidi-bel-Abbès in October 1962.*

Another unit had also been created in February 1940: the 13th Foreign Legion [Mountain] Half-Brigade (13th DBLE), commanded by Lieutenant-colonel Magrin-Vernerey. It had been intended at first to send this unit to Finland, to help fight the Soviet invasion. Delays in training and government vacillation put paid to this plan, and in the end it was sent to Norway – a strangely arctic destination for a unit formed on the sands of North Africa.

Embarking at Brest on 22 April 1940, the 13th DBLE reached Liverpool on 25 April, departing four days later to arrive, on 6 May, at Ballangen, the advanced base for operations at Narvik. At dawn on 13th May, the Legionnaires landed on the soil of Norway. In a matter of hours,

the 1st Battalion took Bjervik, the 2nd Battalion, Moeby. The next day, a patrol destroyed German aircraft based on Lake Hartvigvand. But the main objective was Narvik, on the other side of Rombakfjord.

This second landing took place on 28 May. The 2nd Battalion climbed the cliffs; hard fighting followed, along the railway track linking Narvik with Sweden, until nightfall saw the 1st Battalion in the heart of Narvik itself. The operation was completely successful, and the days which followed saw the Germans driven back to the frontier. They were saved, at the last moment, by the German offensive in France. Paris needed all her troops, and the Legionnaires had to reembark in haste. By 6 June, it was all over.

After spending several days trying to organize a defensive position in Brittany (the 'Breton redoubt'), the 13th DBLE found itself once again climbing the gangplanks at Brest, and crossing to England. There it was offered a choice: either to continue the fight under General de Gaulle, alongside the British, or to return to Morocco. The 2nd Battalion, whose commander, Guéninchault, had been killed at Narvik, and in which the influence of the Georgian Prince, Capitaine Amilakvari, was strong, chose Free France. The 1st Battalion preferred repatriation to North Africa.

On 31 August, the 'dissidents' (who had provisionally awarded themselves the title of 14th Half-Brigade, but who soon reverted to 13th DBLE) embarked once more in England. Their destination was Africa. After a check before Dakar, which remained loyal to Pétain, the Legionnaires sailed right round the south of Africa. Their first operation was against the Italians in Eritrea where, on 8 April 1941, they took the port of Massawa from a garrison of fourteen thousand enemy troops. But it was in the Western Desert that the real glory awaited the Legionnaires of the 13th DBLE.

BIR HAKEIM

Initially, the 1st Free French Brigade (in which the 13th DBLE now served, two battalions strong) was assigned to an attack on Halfaya Pass in January 1942. They arrived too late. The headquarters of the British 8th Army, to which the brigade was attached, sent them next to help in the construction of the defensive Gazala Line. They were posted to the most southerly point of the line, the 'box' named Bir Hakeim.

Bir Hakeim was the 'desert of the desert' – utterly desolate. For three months, the Legionnaires and their comrades from the colonies laid out defences and dug in. They knew that the German Afrika Korps and the Italians who faced them were preparing for an offensive. This was unleashed on 27 May 1942. Rommel planned to take Tobruk and then to drive on towards Alexandria. He had everything to gain; but he had not counted on the frenzied resistance of the French at Bir Hakeim, which cost him ten days. Those ten days were precious: they allowed the 8th Army to fall back in relatively good order, and to regroup on the El Alamein Line.

To describe the fighting at Bir Hakeim would be to describe hell: fire, steel, dust, flies – and thirst, that old familiar companion of the Legionnaires from the Sahara. On the night of 10 June, their mission fulfilled, the French fought their way out of the strongpoint and regrouped to the east, at the southern end of the Alamein Line.

At the beginning of November 1942, the Americans landed in Morocco; the second front in the west had opened. A few days earlier, on 23 October, Montgomery had opened his attack from the Alamein Line. The Legion's mission was to

Bren-gun carriers of the 13th DBLE in Libya, 1942.

The 13th DBLE embarking at Brest for Norway, April 1940.

take the plateau of El Himeimat on the edge of the Qattara Depression. It was there, at 9.30 a.m. on 24 October, that Colonel Amilakvari, now commander of the 13th DBLE, was killed.

Re-formed during the following winter, the 13th DBLE took part in the advance to Tunisia in early 1943. There they met their brothers-in-arms, the Legionnaires from Algeria, who had returned to the fray at the end of 1942, attacking the Axis forces from the Algerian frontier.

TUNISIA

Shortly after the American landings, the French Army of Africa had mobilized, and prepared to take up the fight again. The Legion was well represented. In December 1942, the 3rd Foreign Infantry Marching Regiment (3rd REIM) was formed; and later, with elements shipped up from garrisons in Senegal, the 1st REIM. The cavalry also formed an independent reconnaissance group; and this was the first unit to see action. On 11 January 1943, it attacked and drove back the enemy at Foum-el-Gouafel, taking two hundred prisoners and thirty 47 mm. guns.

A few days later, the 3rd REIM, operating alongside the British in the direction of Djebel Mansour, clashed hard against Von Arnim's tanks. French equipment – even the much newer equipment of the Americans – was no match for Tiger tanks, and the 3rd REIM suffered heavy casualties. But the Legionnaires had their revenge. In April, the allies advanced and, on 9 May, the 3rd REIM took Zaghouan. By the time of the cease-fire on 11 May, the regiment had already taken some five thousand prisoners. The whole of Africa was liberated; now all eyes turned towards Europe.

ITALY

Reorganized and brought up to strength in personnel and equipment, the men of the 13th DBLE embarked for Italy at the end of April 1944. They arrived late in the campaign; they knew it, and were eager to make up for lost time. General Juin would give them their opportunity.

From 13 to 22 May, from San Giorgio to the Liri, the Legion was in the thick of the fighting to pierce the

Top: *A company of the 1st REIM attacking a position in Tunisia in 1943.* Above: *Legionnaires of the 1st REC, with new equipment in Tunisia in 1943, preparing to play their part in the liberation of France.*

Colonial helmet of Rommel's Afrika Korps from the time of the Battle of Bir Hakeim, 1942. Right: *Legionnaire in Tunisia, 1943.*

Adolf Hitler Line. By 25 May, it was done: the way was clear to Rome. After a brief respite in the Eternal City, the 13th DBLE went back into the line on 15 June. Two days later it ran up against the enemy before Radicofani. This battle was crowned by a difficult but decisive victory. The road to Lake Bolzano lay open, and on 3 July the French entered Siena.

Nevertheless, Italy remained a secondary front. A month earlier, on 6 June 1944, the British and Americans had landed in Normandy. It was clear that it was in France that the real campaign of liberation, promising final victory, was now beginning.

On 16 August 1944, at 6 p.m., the 13th DBLE landed at Cacalaire in the south of France. The next day, it cleared the Hyères salt-marshes and the area of Carqueiranne, taking more than three hundred prisoners. Then, after the liberation of Toulon, the Legionnaires started a mad dash to the north in the direction of Autun, where they captured a column of three thousand Germans. (Shortly before reaching Belfort, the 13th DBLE 'incorporated' into its ranks a complete battalion of White Russians serving in the Wehrmacht.)

At the end of December 1944, the 13th DBLE was pulled out of the drive to the east and sent to reduce the stubborn German pockets of resistance which had been holding out on the Atlantic coast since August. Returning to Alsace, the 13th took part in the defence of Strasbourg, and subsequently in the taking of Colmar. There it fought side by side with the RMLE – the reborn Foreign Legion Marching Regiment of 1915–18, now reconstituted from the garrisons of North Africa to fight once again in a battle for France. Alongside the RMLE in the new 5th Armoured Division was the 1st REC, equipped with American armour.

The rancour of the past was forgotten; the Legionnaires of Bir Hakeim fought shoulder to shoulder with their brothers from Africa. In January 1945, in a new departure, the 13th DBLE revived their original 'mountain' tradition and moved into the Alps to take part in the reconquest of the Authion massif, stubbornly held by the Italians. It was there that the cease-fire of 8 May 1945 found them.

FROM ORAN TO THE ARLBERG

Since the end of the fighting in Tunisia in May 1943, the French Army of Africa had been preparing itself for the reconquest of Europe. It was poor in equipment; what was sufficient for the rebels of South Oran province would hardly do for a modern war. It was therefore taken under the wing of the US Army, which equipped, armed and organized it to American standards. Five divisions were formed, of which three – the 1st, 2nd and 5th – were armoured. The Legion formed the backbone of the 5th Armoured Division, with the reconstituted RMLE providing its mechanized infantry and

the 1st REC part of its armoured cavalry. This process took some time, and the 5th Armoured Division was not ready for combat until the early weeks of September 1944. The Legionnaires had to wait until General de Lattre de Tassigny's attack towards Belfort at the beginning of November before they saw combat at last. There followed a long, hard fight through the Vosges in Upper Alsace during the cruel winter of 1944.

Around Christmas, the progress achieved by the German offensive in the Ardennes threatened Strasbourg; then, in January 1945, came the furious fighting for the liberation of Colmar. Each little Alsatian village became a battlefield, to be taken in hand-to-hand fighting. The Wehr-

Legionnaire of the RMLE dressed for the winter campaign for the liberation of France, 1944–45.

macht resisted stubbornly to protect the western frontier of the Reich. On 27 January 1945, Colmar was liberated. The Alsace campaign was over; and in the spring the campaign for Germany began.

The Legion drove on, recording new victories at Karlsruhe, Pforzheim and Stuttgart; but the cavalcade was nearly over. On 25 April 1945, the Legionnaires reached the Danube. They pushed on towards Lake Constance, and at Friedrichshafen they captured the garrison of 1250 men without firing a shot. On 6 May, the 1st Battalion of the RMLE reached the Arlberg. It went no farther: Germany had surrendered.

The crowning glory came in Paris with the parade of 18 June 1945. In the days that followed, the Legion's regiments began to make their way back to North Africa. They hoped for a rest; but they did not get one. Another war was awaiting them – 7500 miles away, in Indo-China.

INDO-CHINA
The storm which had ripped across Europe for five years had not spared the Far East. Allied to the Axis, Japan had pounced on Asia, all the way from Korea to the East Indies by way of China, Burma and Malaya. In 1940, Japan's ally Thailand had attempted a full-scale conquest of Cambodia, which the French forces had vigorously resisted, first sinking the Thai fleet and then maintaining the borders of the French Empire intact. Japan had imposed its 'mediation', however, and had forced France to accept annexation of the western provinces of Cambodia; the territory up to the Mekong River in Laos was handed over to Thailand.

The Legion had been represented in Indo-China since the conquest of the previous century. Since 1930, its units had been gathered into a single regiment, the 5th REI – the most important unit of European troops in the territory. Its usual garrison was in Upper Tonkin, on the edge of the Red River delta. Since the Thai invasion, however, one battalion had been detached to the south, and had taken part in the defeat of the enemy offensive. At that point, on the Chinese border with Upper Tonkin, the vanguard of the Japanese Emperor's 'Army of Canton' began to make its

Legionnaires of the RMLE returning to North Africa in 1945.

presence felt.

The Japanese moved south, falling on the garrison of Lang Son and on a whole string of other posts held by colonial troops – notably, Dong Dang. Hoping to push further, they then advanced on the pass of Dong Mo, held by three battalions of the 5th REI. The expected confrontation never took place. Admiral Decoux, the French commander-in-chief, signed a protocol with the Japanese which spared Indo-China, for a time, from the horrors of a harsh occupation. The French forces in Indo-China were small, and their equipment outdated. Their only resource lay in the quality of the men.

That quality would be proved on 9 March 1945, when the Japanese launched surprise attacks all over the peninsula, obliterating, in a matter of hours, the entire French presence. At Ha Giang, the Legionnaires of the garrison were massacred rather than accept surrender. At Lang Son, Lieutenant Duronsoy's motorized platoon was wiped out. At Tong, the captured Legionnaires were beheaded with swords. Happily, three battalions of the 5th REI were able to form up together and, with the aid of native units, undertook a fighting retreat towards friendly territory in China. The retreat lasted two months, and entered legend as a death-march.

On 15 August 1945, Japan surrendered. French troops were already on their way to Indo-China,

hoping to drive out the army of the Rising Sun. Instead, they found themselves face to face with a popular nationalist insurrection, partly directed by the communists Ho Chi Minh and Vo Nguyen Giap. This new war would drag on for nine years.

To recount in a few lines the events of those nine long years is obviously impossible. The Legion's story is inseparably interwoven with the history of the war, since the Legion alone provided forty per cent of the European troops who took part. Here, too, the casualty figures speak for themselves: no fewer than 309 officers, 1082 *sous-officiers* and 9092 légionnaires lost their lives in the Indo-China campaigns.

Never since its creation had the Foreign Legion put such numbers into the field. There were four regiments of infantry, a regiment of armoured cavalry and its associated amphibious groups, and two battalions of paratroopers, without counting the many independent companies – engineer, transport, repair and maintenance, air re-supply: about thirty thousand men in all.

The 5th REI, exhausted by its ordeal and without relief since 1940, left Indo-China for a while. It was replaced by the 2nd REI, which was based in Central Annam. Next to arrive was the 13th DBLE, and then the 1st REC. The 3rd REI, which soon followed, was the retitled RMLE of the Second World War. After being rebuilt in Algeria, the 5th REI returned in 1949. Each of these regiments fielded two, three, even five battalions in some cases; and as part of General de Lattre's programme for the creation of an effective Vietnamese army, each at one stage incorporated one or two locally recruited battalions under Legion commanders and junior leaders.

In 1948, the Legion's 1st Foreign Parachute Battalion (1st BEP) was formed, followed soon afterwards by the 2nd BEP. These two parachute battalions would cover themselves with glory. Re-formed after being wiped out for the first time in October 1950, the 1st BEP would be joined by its junior sister-unit for its second death at Dien Bien Phu in 1954.

From 1947, the 3rd REI took part in the reconquest of the 'High

Region' of Tonkin – Lang Son, Dong Khe and Bac Khan. It settled down there, building outposts and reassuring the terrorized local population, who depended on the regiment for protection. The Viet Minh reacted by attacking the outposts. Several of them fell; others resisted successfully. This was the case at Phu Tong Hoa, where, on 25 July 1948, the 104 Legionnaires of the 2nd Company, led by Capitaine Cardinal, held off the attacks of two enemy regiments for

more than nine hours. In the morning, the survivors counter-attacked, and cleared the outpost. Two officers and twenty-one légionnaires were killed; but, like their predecessors at Tuyen Quang, the garrison turned out a neatly uniformed guard of honour to present arms to the relief column when it finally arrived.

After January 1950, the defeat of Chiang Kai-shek's Nationalist forces gave the Chinese People's Army access to the border with Indo-China.

From that point on, the Viet Minh enjoyed sanctuaries and arsenals out of reach of the French. The communists took advantage of this opportunity to organize regular units, partly equipped with material abandoned by the Chinese Nationalists, and partly with American equipment captured by the Red Chinese in Korea.

It was clear that enemy pressure would increase along the chain of little forts strung out across the frontier zone on the line of Colonial Road 4 (RC 4) from Lang Son – the name occurs again – to Cao Bang. The crisis came in October 1950. The 3rd REI was ordered to abandon Cao Bang and to fall back along the RC 4 to link up with a supporting column which was moving westwards to meet it. These orders took no account of General Giap.

He prepared an enormous ambush in the steep limestone hills, covered with thick jungle, which dominate every twist of the RC 4 as it snakes its way southeast. Some thirty thousand men were committed to this operation – ten times the strength of the available French forces. And when, on 1 October 1950, the order reached the III/3rd REI to leave its fortified position at Cao Bang, the battalion advanced into a massacre. The so-called 'relief column' was already in serious difficulty itself: attacked from all sides, it was encircled at the bottom of a wooded gorge at Coc Xa, and this despite the emergency support of the paras of the 1st BEP. By the night of 8 October, almost the entire French force had

Top: *The 2nd REI under attack south of Nam Dinh, December 1952.* Above: *The grenade-launcher section of the 1st BEP in action in 1952.* Right: *Legionnaire of the 1st BEP after landing in a rice field in the Tonkin Delta.*

been put out of action – dead, missing or captured. Among the fallen were Commandant Forget, one of the greatest figures of the 3rd REI, and Capitaine Segrétain, the heroic commander of the annihilated 1st BEP.

In January 1951, encouraged by this success, Giap hoped to take Hanoi, the capital of Tonkin. He came up against a man stronger than himself: General de Lattre, who gathered his best units from all over Indo-China – and particularly the 13th DBLE from the far south – to counter Giap's move at Vinh Yen.

The year 1951 brought a succession of victories. Giap was defeated three times: at Mao Khe, where he was faced by tanks and by Legionnaires of the 5th REI; on the Day River, where he came up against the 13th DBLE; and at Nghia Lo, in October 1951, where he fought the paras of the 2nd BEP. The winter which followed saw the great battle of Hoa Binh, in which both the 5th REI and the 13th DBLE distinguished themselves.

In October 1952, Giap put aside his ambition to take the 'High Region'. He concentrated southwards, taking the Nghia Lo ridge between the Red and Black Rivers. Made over-confident by this victory, he threw one of his regular divisions against an isolated French 'airhead' at Na San. The attack began late in November 1952. The communists assaulted Strongpoint 24, unaware that it was held by the 3rd REI, which, since Cao Bang, had a score to settle. Three days of bloody fighting brought the Legionnaires their vengeance, and victory.

A year later, the French began to install a similar, though larger, garrison at Dien Bien Phu. The parachute units which, in November 1953, made the drop to capture this bowl surrounded by hills included the 1st BEP, and a newly formed parachute company of 120 mm. mortars (which the present writer had the honour to command in April 1954). Some of the paratroopers were then replaced by infantry flown in by transport aircraft. On the eve of the enemy assault, in March 1954, five of the ten infantry battalions at Dien Bien Phu were provided by the Legion: the I/13th

Heavy Mortar Company of the 1st BEP in action at Dien Bien Phu.

DBLE, III/13th DBLE, I/2nd REI, III/3rd REI and 1st BEP.

At 5 p.m. on the afternoon of 13 March, Giap launched his offensive. He could field three divisions of infantry (the 308th, 312th and 316th) and a complete division of artillery (the 351st): about fifty thousand men altogether, supplied by some 75,000 to 100,000 coolies. The garrison which faced him numbered just over eleven thousand men, including non-combatants.

The first battalion to be attacked was the III/13th DBLE, dug in on strongpoint 'Béatrice'. In a matter of hours, the battalion lost all its officers, including Commandant Pégot and Capitaine Pardi. Colonel Gaucher was soon to follow them. At 1 a.m. the next morning, submerged by a tide of enemies, the 250 survivors on 'Béatrice' were overrun.

The days which followed were no better. Despite parachute drops into the perimeter by five more airborne battalions, including the 2nd BEP, and by numerous untrained volunteers who came to fight along-

side their comrades, the garrison of Dien Bien Phu was forced to cease fire on 7 May 1954. The last unit left fighting was the III/3rd REI at strongpoint 'Isabelle', which was overrun at dawn on 8 May.

ALGERIA

Early in September 1954, at Tuyen Quang, close to the monument erected in 1930 to the heroes of Dominé's siege in 1885, a Viet Minh political commissar announced to a group of Legion prisoners from Dien Bien Phu that 'the next stage of the decolonization process will take place in North Africa'.

He was speaking no more than the truth. Since 1 November 1953, armed groups of the Algerian National Liberation Army (ALN) had been mounting a series of terrorist outrages in Constantine province. The Algerian War had begun. It was to last for six-and-a-half years.

Hardly off the ships from Indo-China, Legionnaires became caught up in the war. It had a particular intimacy for them: they were defending

Motorized section of the 4th REI in difficulties near Biskra, Algeria, in 1958. Top: *Colonel Jeanpierre, commanding the 1st REP, shortly before his death in 1958.*

Top: *Colonel Favreau, commanding the 5th REI, inspects his regiment on operations in Algeria in 1959.* Above: *Camerone Day parade of the 2nd REI at Aïn Sefra.*

their homeland. It was here that they had first taken up arms, 123 years before.

The Legion's effective strength was more or less the same as it had been in Indo-China, with the exception of the Vietnamese auxiliary units which had been left behind. The 1st RE continued to provide depot services and training for the Legion as a whole, at its centres at Sidi-bel-Abbès, Saïda and Mascara. The other units involved were the 2nd, 3rd, 4th and 5th REI and the 13th DBLE; the two parachute battalions, which were soon reorganized as regiments designated 1st and 2nd REP; the 1st and 2nd REC; and the four Saharan Motorized Companies (CSPL) which patrolled the oil-rich sands of the far south. The total strength was around twenty thousand men.

In general terms, the Algerian War consisted of a succession of encounters with small armed bands, which occasionally broke the monotony of long weeks of marches, sweeps and ambushes in search of intelligence. With few exceptions, there were no real 'battles' to leave their names in the record, as had been the case in Indo-China. One of the exceptions was the 'Battle of the Frontiers' in the course of which, near Souk Ahras in April 1958, the 1st REP's Colonel Jeanpierre was killed.

Although the enemy units presented an impression of organization in the early months of the war, they never managed to create a battlefield force analogous to that which General Giap had fielded from 1950 onwards. The Legion and other French units invariably came up against ALN groups of limited size, seldom larger than a *katiba* – a strong company of about 150 to 180 *fellagha*. After General Challe's large-scale operations in 1959, the French never again encountered more than the remnants of armed gangs, forced to revert once more to the terrorist methods of before 1955.

The terrain of Algeria is of unparalleled difficulty for the soldier. Oran province remained calm for a long time, and most of the skirmishes took place in the eastern part of the country, notably in three particular areas. These were the massif of the Aurès and Nementchas, on the edge of the Sahara, where the 3rd REI, 1st REC and 4th REI served successively; the frontier zone from Bône down to Khenchela, where the 1st and 2nd REP and the 2nd REC operated; and the 'Triangle' of the Collo-Djidjelli peninsula, heavily wooded, cut by gorges and riddled with caves – altogether an ideal refuge for the

A Sikorsky helicopter drops a section of the 4th CSPL close to the Moroccan border in the Algerian Sahara in October 1959. Below: Light armoured car of the 1st REC on observation duties near an Algerian shrine in 1958.

rebels. This area was the domain of the 3rd REI from 1956 onward.

To the west, towards Oran and Mostaganem, the 5th REI based itself at Arzew; while the 2nd REI fought in the south, after returning in 1956 from a spell in Morocco.

For six years, white képis and green berets were to be seen in every part of the country. By the end of the campaign, the Legion had lost 65 officers, 278 *sous-officiers* and 1633 légionnaires dead. This may have been only a fifth of the losses in Indo-China, but, for the Legion, the loss of Algeria itself would be more serious in another way. It was a bitter, divisive experience; and the general feeling was that not enough had been done to hold on to the

Mujaheddin cap, epaulettes, badges and fellagha *insignia of rank found by the 1st Battalion of the 5th REI in the course of operations in the Turenne region of Algeria.*

wars, is on the way to achieving its titanic task of driving the 'Route de l'Est ('Eastern Highway') through the jungle. In the islands of the Pacific, the 5th Mixed Pacific Regiment (5th RMP) has built France's nuclear test facilities; the regimental trumpet-banners still bear the old motto 'Régiment du Tonkin'. In Djibouti, the 13th DBLE – the regiment of Narvik, Bir Hakeim and Dien Bien Phu – guarantees almost single-handedly, the security of the young republic. Whether it be currently on Mayotte, until recently in Corsica, yesterday at Aubagne and Castelnaudary, or tomorrow at Nîmes – everywhere, the Legion builds. In the spirit of their forefathers, Legionnaires still build everything to last for ever, thus laying the foundations for the future.

Sadly, that future will perhaps also hold war. The Legion is prepared for it. Its intervention regiments have proved, on several occasions during the past twenty years, that they are among the best troops in the world. This has been demonstrated at Kolwezi; and it has been demonstrated, on several occasions, in Chad.

CHAD, 1969–1980
In 1969, the legal government of Chad, then in the hands of the Negro, non-Muslim people of this ethnically divided country, was fighting against two rebel movements, inspired and supported from outside its borders. One of these movements was based on Chad's eastern frontier, and President Tombalbaye accused it of operating from Sudanese bases. The other, built around a Tubu tribal party, was more active in the central Saharan areas; its range extended to the Libyan frontier and skirted the Ennedi and Borkou massifs, which rise in great, desolate slabs from the middle of the desert.

Between April and September 1969, three companies of the 2nd REP left Calvi (the parachutists' base in Corsica) for Fort Lamy, commanded by Colonel Lacaze. They were accompanied by a composite Motorized Company (the CMLE), formed from personnel of the non-paratroop units of the Legion and led by Capitaine Aubert. These four companies, grouped under two tactical headquarters (Combat Groups Chastenet and Malaterre), established

territory. There had been no lack of human courage; only of political will. In 1961, when the imminent abandonment of Algeria became clear, the Legion asked itself some hard questions about the meaning that should be given to the words inscribed on its colours: 'Honour and Fidelity'. The mutiny which broke out in April 1961 engulfed, among other units, the 1st REP, which was subsequently disbanded for the third time.

THE LEGION LIVES ON
In 1962, the French Army left Algeria and returned to France. The Foreign Legion had no other home than Sidi-bel-Abbès. It found itself in the same dilemma as the million European Algerians driven out of the country of their birth: without family, without roots. More than any other group, the Legion had built Algeria, and had

impressed its seal upon it. The best illustration of this feeling is, perhaps, the inscription left engraved on the walls of the post of Djenien Bou Rezg by Legionnaires of the 6th Motorized Company of the 2nd REI, before leaving their buildings to the Algerians: 'Soldiers of the People's National Army – The camp of Djenien Bou Rezg is the work of men of the Foreign Legion. Keep this valuable benefit intact for your country, this testimony to the nobility of men.'

For more than twenty years now, the Legion has lived on. In the four corners of the earth, Legionnaires still fulfil one of the great missions that has always been theirs: opening roads and marking tracks, constructing installations of every kind, and developing the countryside. In French Guiana, the 3rd REI, heir to the famous RMLEs of two world

Chad, 1970. Top: *Colonel Lacaze, commanding the 2nd REP, inspects a detachment of his regiment.* Above: *Two columns of the 2nd REP meet on a track during operations against the rebels.*

bases in the bush at Mongo and Am-Timan, within the rebels' operational zones.

Motorization in all-terrain vehicles, combined with helicopter transport, gave these companies a high standard of efficiency in a mission which could easily have become confused and incoherent: alertness and accurate information were essential. Little by little, the rebel gangs were worn down; enemy raids became

rare, along the banks of the Chari as much as in the valleys of the eastern tributaries. The Legionnaires operated in an environment of scrubby bush, parched grassland, marshes and muddy tracks, in a climate that was always hot and often humid. But their continual sweeps did not prevent them from cementing good relations with the inhabitants of the thatched villages, who were attached to their traditional way of life and

were accustomed, after nearly thirty years, to the sight of French soldiers.

By early 1971, the central and southern areas of Chad could be described as pacified. The attention of the high command now focused on the north. The 'fox-hunting' sport was over; now it was more like following a wild boar into its lair. The often very unequal encounters of the past year were forgotten in violent clashes with whole rebel gangs, who had to be ferreted out of their hide-outs on the slopes of rocky terrain, which served them both as observation post and fortress. Most of the Legion's casualties in Chad were suffered in the course of these actions. In December 1971, the CMLE and 2nd REP returned to Corsica: their task had been accomplished to the declared satisfaction of President Tombalbaye.

Nevertheless, in 1978, Chad was again torn by such disorder that the government renewed its call to France for the military aid laid down in the treaty of cooperation. In May, the Legion departed once more for Fort Lamy, now rechristened N'Djamena. The intervention group comprised a squadron of light armour from the 1st REC, and a company of the 2nd REI from southern Corsica. The Legionnaires based themselves at Atti, and spread out from there on a series of policing and security operations which lasted several months.

The military situation had

changed in the past seven years. The enemy was much stronger than before, both in skills and in equipment. The French combat group was supported by modern aircraft such as the Jaguar and Bréguet Atlantic. Legion personnel were relieved at regular intervals by new drafts of troops from their parent units. This rotation of companies ensured a continually high standard of fitness in an exhausting climate; but it did present problems from the standpoint of maintaining continuity of local knowledge. Such detailed local intelligence is vital in a war in which it is hard to tell today's friend from yesterday's foe, and vice versa.

The struggle for power was soon visible on the streets of the capital itself. The Legion combat group now concentrated on N'Djamena, where it became increasingly involved in the protection of French lives and property, while simultaneously filling the uncomfortable role of arbiter and buffer between various factions. In April 1980, the Legion pulled out of Chad and returned to France, to await further missions. As these lines were being written, the 2nd REP was packing its kitbags yet again: destination, Chad.

KOLWEZI, 1978

At dawn on 13 May 1978, the mining town of Kolwezi, in Shaba province of southern Zaïre, was seized by the kind of madness and violence that the three thousand European residents believed to be a thing of the distant past. The Katanga secession crisis, sparked off by Moïse Tshombe, was a dim memory, and the central government assured its authority by the presence of troops of the Zaïrean regular army. But when the shooting started on that already stifling dawn, the Zaïrean troops scattered almost without a fight – and left the population, black and white, to the mercy of the Katangan 'Tiger' rebels.

They came from nearby Angola to reconquer their province. They were heavily armed, but did not concern themselves with either strategy or tactics. They simply put Kolwezi to the sack, pillaging the stores, wrecking the houses, drinking anything they could lay hands on, raping and murdering indiscriminately.

In Kinshasa, the directors of the Gécamines mining company were warned of the situation by the radio operator at Kolwezi, who was still able to transmit at that stage. At first, they simply prayed that the rebels would soon drift away. When this hope proved vain, they turned to the French ambassador and to Colonels Larzul and Gras, respectively the French military attaché and the head of the technical assistance team. These officers passed on the appeal to the Western powers, and even outlined a possible scheme for a rescue mission led by troops from Europe.

On 17 May, convinced that the European residents of Kolwezi were in deadly danger, and impatient at the procrastinations of the Belgian government, the French government decided to intervene. The 2nd REP, stationed at Calvi in Corsica, was put on stand-by. Companies dispersed on exercise, and individuals absent on courses, were recalled at once. By the end of that afternoon, the commander, Colonel Erulin, could report that his regiment was ready. He received his movement order at 1.30 a.m. on 18 May. Operation 'Leopard' had begun.

An enormous distance separated Solenzara airfield in Corsica from the objective in Shaba province. It would take eight hours by jet airliner to reach Kinshasa, and another four hours in the paratroop transports from the capital to Kolwezi. The time available for preparing the operation was cut to the bone: even a rumour of the forthcoming 'drop' – which was hard to keep secret, under the circumstances – might be the signal for a general massacre of the Europeans.

By 11.30 p.m. the same day, 18 May, Colonel Erulin was in Kinshasa. Without much respect for the original flight plan, the five DC-8s bringing his 650 paratroopers arrived during the course of that night. The force comprised a headquarters, a reconnaissance platoon, a mortar platoon and four rifle companies.

Despite having to overcome such technical difficulties as breakdowns among the C-130 transports, and the incompatibility of the paratroopers' personal equipment with the American parachutes which were issued to them on the spot, the first of two 'lifts' took off from Kinshasa at 11 a.m. on 19 May. Arriving over Kolwezi at 3 p.m., the six C-130s dropped the headquarters and three companies of the 2nd REP from a height of six hundred feet.

They were met by the fire of automatic weapons, but the paras quickly silenced these as soon as they reached the ground. Forming up on

Colonel Erulin, commanding the 2nd REP, directs operations in Kolwezi in May 1978.

the dropping zone, they moved off towards their assigned objectives. After a frustrating advance through an area of enclosed gardens and yards, under sporadic harassing fire from the scattered Katangans, the 'Green Berets' cleared and occupied the Old Town. Everywhere lay decomposing corpses, among wrecked and burnt-out bungalows. By nightfall, several score of the hostages taken by the fanatical rebels had been set free. Several hundred other Europeans could see the end of their nightmare approaching. But progress was slower in the New Town: the 'Tigers' were still patrolling this area in armoured vehicles, while the Legionnaires were on foot. Several brief encounters showed the skill and cold-blooded courage of the REP weapons crews; and the destruction of two Katangan armoured cars at an important road junction cooled the enemy's enthusiasm.

At dawn on 20 May, while the second wave of paras jumped in their turn and proceeded to settle things in the New Town, one company managed to penetrate the native quarter of Manika, clearing it house by house. The Legionnaires rescued many hostages, in the nick of time, from the last bands of armed rebels, who were already beginning to shoot them out of hand.

For the first time in a very long week, calm began to settle over Kolwezi. The population was able to come out into the daylight, to exchange news and to count the cost. It was heavy. Wherever they went, the Legionnaires found bodies – lying alone, or piled in charnel-houses: tortured, burned, hacked to pieces in evidence of a blind savagery. The shocked European residents needed no persuasion to leave their town the following morning by air, at the urging of the Belgian troops, who had finally arrived and taken over the airfield.

But if his regiment had successfully regained control of Kolwezi town in a matter of hours, Colonel Erulin was under no illusion that the rebellion was over. He sent out fighting patrols into the housing estates which lay around the town. At the Metal-Shaba site, some three miles north of the New Town, the Legionnaires fought a sharp engagement against several companies of Katangan 'Tigers', solidly dug in and heavily armed – an action which cost the regiment four more lives. The assault went in after a heavy mortar barrage; the enemy was forced to withdraw, leaving behind many dead, as well as quantities of weapons, including mortars, machine guns and recoilless cannons.

Between 21 and 27 May, using both their own vehicles flown in by transport aircraft and others provided by Gécamines, the 2nd REP extended the range of its patrols. Resistance crumbled; the enemy had cut and run for the Angolan frontier. Between 28 May and 8 June, Colonel Erulin redeployed his men between Kolwezi and the provincial capital of Lumumbashi, whose inhabitants needed a gesture of reassurance. Confidence soon revived.

When the African Multi-National Force landed in Shaba on 8 June, the 2nd REP was able to return to its base in Corsica with the satisfaction of

Kolwezi, 1978. The 2nd REP preparing for the drop. Opposite: *Evacuating a wounded civilian.*

having accomplished its rescue mission, at a cost of five dead and twenty-five wounded, and with an efficiency and dash that had earned the regiment a world-wide reputation.

LEBANON, 1982–1983

When it was decided, in September 1982, to send a multi-national peace-keeping force to Beirut, the French government turned once more to the 2nd REP. With the coolness of professional soldiers, and the Legion's customary discipline and vigilance, the regiment kept tight control of the harbour during the difficult period of the PLO fighters' evacuation by sea, and carried out observation and patrol duties in the western area of the city.

In the spring of 1983, the Western governments decided to send a new peace-keeping force back into Beirut; and again the Legion was

represented. This time, it was under the orders of the 31st Brigade, commanded by General Coullon, who was also the commander of the Foreign Legion Group (GLE) – the overall Legion operational and administrative headquarters. It was the turn of the 'Green Berets' of the 2nd REI, 1st RE and 1st REC to experience the difficult task of keeping the peace. The press declared that 'only soldiers like these could endure, with undiminished discipline, the sniping, shelling and casualties which are their daily lot'. In its three-month stay in the Lebanon, the Legion added to its long roll of honour the names of five men killed and twenty-five wounded.

Thus, in the course of 153 years of history, the Foreign Legion has served France – and often, through her, the cause of the free world. The

uniforms and the theatres of operation have changed, to be sure. Today, recognized as a crack force, the Legion has become a spearhead, thoroughly expert in the most modern techniques and in the use of the most up-to-date weapons.

The spirit of the Legion, that mixture of hardness and generosity, is still the same as ever. Trained for combat to the most demanding standard, and confident of his worth, the Legionnaire carries out his orders without hesitation – and without flinching from the sacrifices that may be necessary. He knows how to build as stylishly as he will face death under fire. This is the heritage that has been handed down, and strengthened, by all those generations who have worn with pride the badge of the seven-flamed grenade – for ever mindful of the motto 'Honneur et Fidélité'.

The 2nd REP in Beirut, August 1982.

The Legion Today.

North African Memories: Sidi-bel-Abbès.

Oran. Algeria's second city and the main port of arrival for thousands of Legionnaires.

We may be living in an age of ever-increasing speed, when the traveller can cross the Atlantic in a few hours, breakfast on the plane, lunch in Manhattan, and be back home for dinner all in the same day—providing he has the stamina, of course. But hiring a car for a few score miles in Algeria can be a problem.

The raven-haired young Arab woman in the Algerian State Tourist Office in Oran's Boulevard Abd-el-Kader was doing her best to find a car, but with little success. 'Perhaps Monsieur could call back in a few hours. By then I may have found a car and a driver for you.' Her English was slow, with an interesting mixture of French and Arabic intonations. I explained that I was only in Oran for a few days and wished to make my journey to Sidi-bel-Abbès as soon as possible.

It was the receptionist at the Royal Hotel who solved the problem. Like hotel receptionists the world over, he knew where to find what guests wanted. Vanishing into the busy street, he reappeared a few minutes later with Mustapha. Unshaven, with what looked like a week's growth of beard, and wearing an old baggy suit, Mustapha explained, in a mixture of Arabic, English and French, that he could take me to Sidi-bel-Abbès. He owned a Volkswagen Passat that he was immensely proud of, assuring me that I would be very comfortable. He would give me an excellent price for the day—900 dinars. I gasped at him in mock horror. With the exchange rate at little more than seven dinars to the pound, this amounted to about £128.00! The Arab sport of haggling began, and finally a price of 550 dinars was agreed. Within ten minutes, we were on our way. Mustapha drove the battered car along the boulevard, turned left through some narrow alleys, on to the main road, past the port, and headed south on to the N 4.

Sidi-bel-Abbès—old Algerian hands will remind you to call it simply Bel-Abbès—is some fifty miles south of Oran, with the minaretted town of Tlemcen to the west and Mascara, a former Legion training centre, to the east. The road is a good one and twin-laned for the first twenty miles or so. The dusty brown landscape rises gently on the journey southwards, broken only from time to time by clumps of scraggy trees and small farms. The little Arab communities make a hard living from the land with crops of olives and grapes, while others tend goats and sheep. At Oued Tielat we turned right on to the N 13, crossed the single-track railway leading to Sig and Mascara, and followed the road south.

Looking out across the dusty landscape, I wondered what misgivings the thousands of Legion recruits may have had who travelled down this same road when Algeria had been a part of France. For me, there was an inner excitement about this journey. It was a pilgrimage that had taken more than twenty years to complete.

It was in November of 1960 that I had first arrived in Algeria, to photograph the conflict there. The French Minister of Defence had, within a week of my arrival, agreed that I could proceed to the Legion's headquarters at Bel-Abbès. This was a sensitive time in the Legion's history. Only a few months later, on 30 April 1961, the Legion's 1st Foreign Parachute Regiment would be disbanded, condemned for its fateful part in the putsch of 21 March that was to leave its mark on France for more

than two decades. Onlookers tell of Legionnaires weeping and throwing their medals on the ground to the cries of *'Vive la Légion! Vive l'Algérie française!'* But my visit to Bel-Abbès was not to be. Months of wandering through Africa, photographing a continent in turmoil, had exhausted me, and I was forced to return to Canada and rest.

The bare, dusty fields, crowned by distant rainclouds from the coastal plain, disappeared, giving way to small industrial buildings on the outskirts of Bel-Abbès. Now the street was lined with trees; a café, hotel, shops and a garage came into view, along with the local townsfolk. It was near midday, and for the inhabitants of Bel-Abbès it was time to eat and pray. Mustapha knew Bel-Abbès well, and parked the car alongside the line of cafés that flanked the town's square. Instantly recognizable was the old bandstand, which I had seen in an early picture in the Legion museum at Aubagne—its white latticed ironwork now neglected and in need of painting. Three Arab children swung from the short flight of steps leading up to its platform. Crossing the square to study the bandstand more closely, I pondered on the days when Legionnaires, with their wives or mistresses, would sit under the trees, drinking their beer and wine to the music of their band. Looking out across the square through the iron latticework, the bandstand seemed sadly out of place. Long since gone were the white képis and bronzed Legionnaires, singing their songs to Véronique and Anne-Marie.

The old Quartier Viénot is only a few minutes' walk from the town square. The former street names had disappeared, following Algerian independence, to be replaced by signs in Arabic, which I found of little help. But Legion friends had provided me with good directions. Turning the corner of one of the narrow streets, the walls of the four-storeyed barracks faced me, immediately familiar from the number of old photographs I had studied in books and at the museum. The ochre-coloured walls stood stark against a bright-blue sky. Gloom and decay encircled the building. Shutters, with their paint peeling, sagged on their hinges against broken windows. Walking under the walls towards the main gate, I wondered if the barracks were deserted and I could possibly gain entrance.

A head appeared through one of the broken windows, wearing a sloppy khaki fatigue cap. So the building was inhabited after all. The boulevard in front of the main gates was narrower than I had expected. Passing on the opposite side of the road, I was now level with the Legion's *Voie Sacrée* (its Sacred Way), so often seen in old photographs of the Quartier. Any indication that the Legion had been there had long since been removed, and now above the gates was the crest of the Algerian army. The sentry stood dejectedly inside his shabby box, ignoring the stranger walking slowly down the other side of the street. Without the Monument aux Morts and its inscription *Honneur et Fidélité*, the square looked naked. At the end of the boulevard I retraced my steps, crossing the road to obtain a closer look at the old buildings. Wild flowers were finding their way through the broken windows that had once been kept so spotlessly clean by Legion recruits. Now there was only silence. Even the Quartier's new inhabitants did not appear to venture here. Level with the gates once more, I looked over the buildings that mysteriously echoed a turbulent past. It was here, on the night of 24 October 1962, that several hundred Legionnaires had stood in silence as two black flags, taken from the Chinese at Tuyen Quang in 1885, were burnt. Capitaine le Vicomte de Borelli had captured the flags during the final days of the battle, and it was his dying wish that, should the Legion ever leave Algeria, the flags would never go to France. By the light of flaming torches, the Legionnaires sang *Le Boudin* as their flag was lowered for the last time. They sang long into the night and, in the pale light of a North African dawn, fifty lorries filled with Legionnaires departed through a silent Bel-Abbès.

As I made my way through the narrow streets, the sound of singing seemed to come from within the walls of the old Quartier. The echo of the Legion's slow, rhythmic march was unmistakable as the proud strains of the Boudin resounded through the town.

> *Au cours de nos campagnes lointaines,*
> *Affrontant la fièvre et le feu,*
> *Nous oublions avec nos peines*
> *La mort qui nous oublie si peu*
> *Nous, la Légion.*

Algeria and the Legion could never be parted.

Traces of the French colonial era can still be found in Sidi-bel-Abbès. Opposite: *The old bandstand.*

53

The Contract: Legion Headquarters at Aubagne.

Aubagne. The Quartier Viénot.

When independence came to Algeria in 1962, the Legion had no option but to uproot itself from Sidi-bel-Abbès. Algeria, home of the Legion for more than a hundred years, had no place for the men with whom so many savage battles had been fought. It was the end of an era, and things would never be the same again. For the first time in its history, the Legion would have its headquarters in mainland France. As Legionnaires wiped the dust of Algeria from their boots, many wondered about their own future as well as that of the Legion. Perhaps this was the end after all? Forgotten by France, and by the politicians in Paris, would they be asked to disappear quietly, never to surface again? It was to the small town of Aubagne, near Marseilles in southern Provence, that they came to lick away the wounds of Algeria and to rebuild their 'home'. During World War Two, the Legion's new headquarters had been used by the German navy, but now the Legion was about to remould its history from the remains of old wooden barracks. The Monument to the Dead, a giant bronze globe of the world, guarded at each corner by four bronze Legionnaires, would be rebuilt, together with a Sacred Way. These would face Algeria and the desert, to be a constant reminder of those who were left behind, for ever buried in the sand.

After the recruiting office, Aubagne is the would-be Legionnaire's first step into the mystical world of the Legion. There are sixteen Legion recruiting centres in various parts of France, from La Citadelle in Lille to the Bas-Fort Saint-Nicolas in Marseilles. Understandably, many young hopefuls for enlistment arrive at Fort de Nogent, a difficult-to-find address in a dreary suburb of Paris. I say 'hopefuls', for, contrary to popular belief, the Legion does not accept everyone who comes knocking at her door. Undoubtedly, during the Legion's early years, very little was asked about the recruit's background. As long as you looked healthy, could carry your pack, and were willing to fight for France, you were in. Today's Legion can be more discriminating. With increasing areas of unemployment in various parts of Europe, and especially in Britain, the Legion is now in a position to choose whom she wants. Aubagne is where the filtering process starts.

A Legionnaire gets to know Aubagne well, with its cafés, bars and pretty girls around the market square. This is where his life in the Legion begins and ends. It was during a visit to one of the Legion's remote overseas postings that I met Dean, who told me how he enlisted. Dean was not his real name, but that is of little consequence, since many Legionnaires take advantage of enlisting under an assumed name. It is part of their purging process, in wanting to forget their past and begin a new life. Dean was British and in his early twenties. His pronounced regional accent would most certainly have puzzled the French, but he was popular and his friends understood him. Brown as a nut and undoubtedly tough, he had a quiet, friendly manner. We talked about how he came to enlist in the Legion. He had written to the French Embassy in London, asking for information, but had received little help. So he packed his bags, told friends he was going to Greece on holiday, and made his way to France. Somehow he found his way to the Legion recruiting office in Lille, with the help of directions on scraps of paper from barmen and his first two words of French, 'Légion Etrangère'. He continued his story with delightful touches of northern English humour. 'I met this corporal in the Citadel in Lille. He spoke a little English, so I explained to him that I wanted to join the Legion. He wanted to know if I had been in prison and all sorts of other personal questions. He took my seaman's papers and my clothes and gave me a track suit. Then I signed a paper for five years in the Legion. I knew that I couldn't marry or own a motorbike or anything like that.' Within the week, Dean was at Aubagne for final selection with a group of thirty others. Three weeks later, he and a Frenchman were the only ones the Legion wanted. 'In Aubagne', he said, 'you're like in a cage. There's people from all over the world there. There's a lot of fights because there's no discipline. All you're doing is waiting. Waiting to get that red band that says you're clear. I think that if you can get through Aubagne you can get through the lot.' (During the three-week selection process, potential recruits are graded by colours: yellow after the first week, green after the second and red for the final week.) He thought back on his first year and came to the opinion that it had been quite an experience. 'You're given a hard time and you can't relax. If you can't take it, you shouldn't have joined in the first place. I've changed a lot since I joined the Legion.'

There are those who embrace the Legion to find themselves, and who look upon their life as a sequence of mental and physical exercises: a kind of Legionnaire's Pilgrim's Progress. James Campbell was such a person. He was a cultured Scot from Edinburgh and would not have been out of place in medical school or a solicitor's office. He had, in fact, once trained to be an accountant. Jim Campbell joined the Foreign Legion in Nice, wearing his grandfather's kilt. You can't be a more loyal Scot than that, and even for the Legion this must have been a first. Five years in the Legion had been good for Jim. He'd found a discipline that appealed to him, regained his self-respect and was a caporal-chef. The Legion was making good use of him in the Statistical Depart-

The Monument aux Morts. Brought from Sidi-bel-Abbès and rebuilt at Aubagne.

ment—a smokescreen name for the internal security operation. Jim interviews most of the Britishers for enlistment. 'They come into my office telling me all sorts of cock-and-bull stories on why they want to join the Legion. I know within a few minutes if they're lying, and tell them to go away and think about it.' Jim had mixed feelings about youngsters with a couple of years on the dole coming into the Legion, and felt that the ex-military men with a 'bit of life under their belts' were preferable. 'A lot of youngsters feel that by joining the Legion they become men—but you don't become a man overnight', he mused.

To ascribe the label of mercenary to today's Legionnaire is to do him an injustice. Understandably, it is a term that he himself despises, and he resents being so referred to by outsiders who have little real knowledge of the modern Legion. There are as many reasons for a man to join the Legion as there are men in it. But, in my experience, they enlist for three basic reasons: to escape from the past and search for a new life; for adventure; and for the attraction of simple military professionalism.

A New Life Begins

In the twenty years that the Legion has been at Aubagne, its home has grown and flourished. But then the Legion has always maintained an air of rigorous élitism, knowing that somewhere within its ranks could be found all the professional skills that it would ever need to draw on.

Recruits arrive at Aubagne from all parts of France to be fed into the selection process. Many potential entrants are surprised at the detailed security checks and medical examinations. The process usually takes about three weeks, and personal clothes, identification papers and passports are taken away – to be returned if the applicant is unsuitable. Dressed in fatigues, and when not required for interviews, the recruit may be given work around the camp to keep him active—for boredom can quickly become an enemy.

In recent years, the selection board has become more demanding. Along with other armies, the Legion is searching for the highest qualifications in education, as well as other skills which give a man a strong military potential.

The recruit will remember Aubagne for two things. It was the place where, for him, a new life began; and, at the end of his contract, it will be the place where he takes his *libération*, bringing his days as a Legionnaire to an end.

A Legionnaire's contract is initially for five years, and it is only after rigorous security and medical checks, taking some weeks, that a potential recruit is considered for training. His passport and personal clothes are taken away and old fatigue uniforms issued.

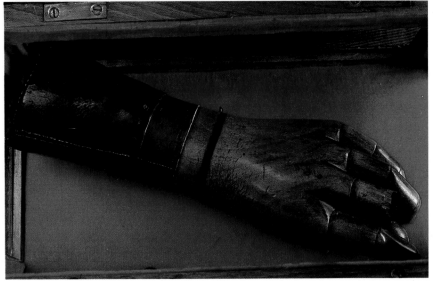

The wooden hand of Capitaine Danjou, killed at the battle of Camerone in 1863, is one of the most precious relics of the Legion. It is kept on the wall of the Legion Crypt (opposite) *and paraded each year on 30 April – Camerone Day.*

The Colonel and His Men

Colonel Forcin gazed through the window of his office overlooking the parade ground at Aubagne. A small group of veterans was laying tributes beside the Legion's Monument to the Dead in the square below. The Colonel paused for a moment, perhaps recalling his own campaigns in Vietnam and Algeria. The red-and-blue decorations on his left breast told their own silent story. Almost a fatherly figure, but with the chiselled face and square body of a prize wrestler, he said: 'A good Legionnaire is a man who needs to find something in the Legion. If he has a past he wants to forget, and needs a lifeline to cling to, and providing he is in good physical condition, he will have the right motivation to succeed with us.'

Colonel R. Forcin, Second-in-Command of the Foreign Legion Group at Aubagne. He is an Officer of the Legion of Honour and is a highly decorated veteran of Vietnam and the Algerian campaigns.

Above right: *General J.-C. Coullon, General Commanding the Foreign Legion Group and the 31st Brigade. He is a Commander of the Legion of Honour and has seen service in Southeast Asia, Algeria and Morocco.* Below right: *Commandant J.-B. Chiaroni (bending over the light box) is Editor-in-Chief of the Legion's monthly magazine, Képi Blanc, and is involved in all aspects of the magazine's production.*

The Bond Is Sealed

The waiting is over. There have been fights and quarrels; days when you thought all the questions and tests would never end; friends you thought would make it have been rejected. Today you are issued with your equipment, *le paquetage*. It is worth about £500 and contains all the personal items and uniform you will need in your five years as a Legionnaire: khaki dress uniform, shoes, boots (*les Rangers*), combat dress, shirts, green ties, overcoat, green beret, badges, red epaulettes, blue waist sash, and the most prized item of all – the white képi.

I watched a thirty-strong group shuffle out of the quartermaster's stores at Aubagne, awkwardly lugging their *paquetage*. They were bound for the Training Regiment at Castelnaudary. Within a few weeks, the rounded shoulders and flabby muscles would be firmly drilled into shape on the 4th Foreign Regiment's parade ground.

To recruits, the clearance period at Aubagne may seem tedious. Perhaps they have not yet realized that it is only the first stage in a readjusted life which they will never forget.

The selection process is over and the Legion recruits are about to depart for the Training Regiment at Castelnaudary. The complete kit (paquetage) has just been issued, containing everything that the Legionnaire will require during his initial five-year contract.

Shaping the Man: Castelnaudary and Beyond.

Castelnaudary. The Quartier Lapasset.

Just off the A 61 between Carcassonne and Toulouse in southern France is the small town of Castelnaudary. It is a classic agricultural community, with a market square, a row of cafés in the main street, and three medium-priced hotels. As well as the beautiful organ in the church of St Michael, and the *cassoulet*, a local dish of meat and beans, the town is also the home of the 4th Foreign Regiment—the Training Regiment of the French Foreign Legion.

Over the years, the Quartier Lapasset at Castelnaudary has had various military uses, though few of them of any significance. Records show that, at the beginning of World War I, it was used as a dispersal point for France's colonial troops. Located in a quiet residential area a few minutes' walk from the town centre, the three-storeyed barracks, with cream-painted walls, red-tiled roofs and neatly pruned trees, radiate a touch of yesterday's army and between-the-wars thinking. The Legion is aware of this and realizes that the old Quartier has a limited future as a training centre. To overcome the confined facilities there, much of the training now takes place in the nearby countryside. To meet future requirements, plans have recently been approved for new quarters, which will be completed within the next few years.

A Legionnaire never forgets 'Castel', where at any one time there may be more than 350 recruits at various stages of training at the 120-year-old Quartier. For almost four months, he is blended into a new life by a team of thirty-five officers and 120 *sous-officiers*, and brought to a peak of physical fitness he may never have thought possible of himself. There are times he would like to forget he ever signed the five-year contract: the cross-country runs that produce aching shoulders from the weight of the pack on his back, and legs that bend like rubber and want to go no further; the sergent bellowing in a language he cannot understand. Most recruits remember it as a terrifying experience.

Sergent Rolls looked down from the third-floor window of the barracks and made a mental note about the squad drilling below. 'The dressing's not bad—not bad at all', he remarked. Rolls was a six-foot Britisher with nearly ten years' service in the Legion. He looked to be in his mid-thirties and had served with the military police in the British army. On the left breast of his khaki tunic he wore the crossed rifles of a marksman. The rolling 'r' made him sound like a Scot, but in fact was the result of earlier years in Canada. 'You have to be tough with recruits', he went on. 'We get very hard men coming into the Legion, and hard men expect hard treatment. That's why they join the Legion. A lot of them have come from orphanages and Borstals and they come into the Legion looking for discipline. If they don't find it, they mess up. They desert, because it's not what they wanted. You see, since the Legion left Algeria, discipline has not been the same, and I feel it's getting to the point where something must be done.'

Later in the day, we met in one of the small bars within walking distance of the Quartier. We talked at great length about the Legion, and tried to reason why men from so many diverse backgrounds turned their backs on the world and disappeared into its ranks. It was a story he told about himself that appealed to me and perhaps gave a clue to his own ideology. While on leave at the family home in a small northern English village, his father sponsored him for membership of an exclusive local club. But Rolls found it was not to his liking. Its members were 'stuffy' and he had little in common with them. After his first visit, much to his father's disappointment, he had no desire to return. They were not his kind of people. 'You see, Dad', he explained, 'I am already in a very exclusive club—so exclusive that money can't get you into it. It's the Foreign Legion. You have to do it off your own bat. Get your balls kicked around your ears, carry your sack, sweat, and when you've got that white képi on your head, you know that no amount of money could buy it.' He took a swig at his Scotch and continued: 'I came into the Legion from the British army, and the only regret I have is that I didn't come in younger; because for me, now, I've found my home. It's the Legion. I don't feel French— no way—but I can't say I feel a hundred per cent British any more.'

After leaving Rolls at the gates of the Quartier, I walked through the damp streets of Castel back to my hotel. A group of Legionnaires was still in one of the bars, their arms around the local girls and oblivious of the hour. Did they also think like Rolls? I wondered.

Each week, a batch of thirty or more recruits— the Legion calls them *engagés volontaires*—passes through the gates of the Training Regiment at Castelnaudary. Apart from their olive-green combat dress, there is little uniformity about the group. The journey by train from Aubagne, where they signed their contracts, will be their last taste of freedom for many weeks. They are now in the Legion and, like it or not, from now on even a beer in the *foyer* will be a privilege.

During his fifteen-week training, a Legionnaire will have improved his running distance from seven to twenty-one kilometres, that is, from less than four and a half to more than thirteen miles. He will be driven even harder. A night run of twenty-five kilometres (fifteen and a half miles) over rough terrain, carrying a fifteen-kilo (thirty-three-pound) pack, must be completed within three hours. He must pass two basic examinations; learn several of the Legion's marching songs; be on guard duty for 192 hours, rotating two hours on and four off; have his hair cut short, but no shorter than seven millimetres (about a quarter of an inch). For this he will receive a maximum of 6816 francs in pay. That is, providing he has not been charged with any offence which has involved being under arrest. Time spent in the guard house is without pay and is added to his contract.

Some recruits never make it. One of two things happens: they desert, or they are discharged as unsuitable for further training. During my several visits to Castelnaudary, I was told that the British can either make the best or the worst Legionnaires. The economic recession in the United Kingdom has led to some training squads now having ten or more 'Brits'. One lieutenant commanding recruits put it this way: 'The British make good Legionnaires and they quickly understand their training, regardless of a poor know-ledge of French. You see, the British are a military people and make good material for the Legion.' On the other hand, there are officers who will tell you that the British make up the highest percentage of deserters.

Sleeping quarters are spartan, with occasional touches of family life.

Austerity and a Sense of Order

The sleeping quarters at the Quartier Lapasset, as in training camps the world over, have little privacy, with some thirty Legionnaires to a dormitory. Beds are bunk-styled and painted battleship grey. Equipment is hung neatly at the foot of the bed; sheets are rolled like sausages and, together with pillows and blankets, form orderly military shapes.

Grey lockers, one to each recruit, line the white-and-cream-walled sleeping areas. On each door is a printed card bearing the recruit's rank and chosen name, while on top stands a pack with a tightly rolled poncho. Inside the locker are neatly pressed khaki shirts and tunics. The white képi has a place of honour on its own shelf, with crossed red epaulettes in front. A sparkling mess tin, bright enough to shave in, with knife, fork and spoon, stands behind. One shelf remains. It is for the few personal items a Legionnaire may have brought with him from his former life—perhaps a picture of his family or of a girlfriend he hopes will wait for him.

The recruit soon learns that there is a Legion way for everything, from pressing the uniforms to cleaning the boots (overleaf). One locker shelf may contain personal items from his former life.

On the blackboard:

FRANCAIS 20.

NOUS AVONS UN BILLET DE 500 F

VOUS AVEZ DES BILLETS

ILS ONT

French in the Classroom

French is the language of the Legion and French classes (above) are now a part of basic training. The common language helps to fashion young men of more than a hundred nationalities into the Legion mould. Right: Uniforms are individually tailored to fit. Overleaf: The recruits' mess hall. Junior NCOs eat with the trainees, who dine on excellent French food with liberal quantities of wine and beer.

Old Legionnaires will tell you that, if you didn't understand a command in their day, you received a crack on the jaw—and then you remembered. Things have changed. In recent years, the Legion has built French lessons into its basic training programme, realizing that, with modern weapons systems, it is essential that orders be instantly understood.

It is not unusual to walk through a barrack block, past one of the classrooms, and to hear recruits repeating elementary French phrases. The Legion has overcome a major teaching problem in communicating to a group of recruits who may, between them, speak ten or more different languages. The teacher uses a system of simple pictures, making his students repeat the French words for the images and objects until they get it right. Sometimes it is a slow process—but it works.

Days That Never Seem to End

Recruits usually arrive over the weekend and are immediately fed into the induction procedure—numerous injections, kit checks, a talk from the Colonel, and a pay advance of a few hundred francs. Their god will be a caporal, whom many will come to hate as their worst enemy on earth. For some, even a letter home, or to a loved one, will be forbidden. If the recruit has come to the Legion for sanctuary, it will protect him; but only if he obeys the Legion's rules. The code of anonymity is sacred to the Legion, and only the individual concerned can break it. For this reason, due warning was always given when I was likely to be photographing, and I asked no questions of anyone who did not wish to answer.

Joe Smoleski, a young Canadian Legionnaire, reasoned it this way: 'A lot of guys join the Legion for the wrong reasons. They have girl problems or, for some reason or other, are unhappy with life. They read a book about the Legion and say, "Wow! That's for me. This tough life is what I need." When they get here, they find it's a different kind of tough—a different kind of mean. When they have to clean their weapons for six hours, or sweep and mop until all they know is floor and broom, they say, "Why have I come here?" They expect to be given a machine gun and a great big target of beer bottles and to fire away. That's not how it goes.... I figure it like this: being a civilian is easy; being a Legionnaire is easy; but the difficulty is the change.' Perhaps Joe was simplifying it a little. I recall seeing Legionnaires on a commando course at Mont Louis, overlooking the Pyrenees, clawing their way through icy water in November. I doubt if they thought it was easy—but I know what he was saying.

Under the keen eye of an adjudant-chef, recruits pound the square at Castelnaudary. Overleaf: *Haircutting in one of the classrooms. The 'boule-zéro' shaven head is now discouraged.*

The Toughening Continues

Mont Louis is ski country. Situated close to Andorra, it offers a bay-window view of the Pyrenees. Inside the small fortress town is the French army's Commando Training School. Here, in recent years, the Legion has carried out its own commando training, run in cooperation with the French army.

Courses at Mont Louis last for several weeks. The natural terrain of the surrounding mountains provides gruelling conditions for the Legion's advanced training. The area immedi-ately around the old fortress—what was once a moat—is now a series of assault courses, designed to exhaust the most spirited of Legionnaires, especially in winter. Commando train-ing at Mont Louis is planned not only to toughen the individual, but to test and train Legionnaires to operate within the framework of a team.

Intensive training tests the Legionnaires to the limits of their endurance. Men of the élite 2nd REP on the assault course at the Mont Louis Commando School.

Strenuous route marches, by day and by night, help to bring Legionnaires to the peak of fitness.

Specialists within the Team

The crossbow is a fearsome weapon—sinister and deadly.

The Legionnaire moved silently through the trees, his green uniform blending into the background of the old fortress and the woods; only the occasional crunch of his footsteps on the light covering of snow betrayed his presence. He fitted the bolt into the crossbow and took aim through the telescopic sight. This was an exercise in the grounds of the Mont Louis Commando School, and one of several specialist roles in which a Legionnaire could be engaged.

At the other side of the fortress, Dave Saunders wriggled under the roll of barbed wire, dragging his submachine gun beside him. His face was scratched and bleeding from a previous 'caper' (as he put it) down a long pipe. The other Legionnaires in the group lay on their backs, holding up the wire with their feet while Dave scrambled through. Watching their progress a few yards away, the two instructors made notes on their teamwork and efficiency. A Glaswegian, with a 'bit of time' in the British army, Dave had found his way into the Legion when he was footloose and tired of Britain. He could not have been more than 5′ 8″, with a chunky frame and tightly cropped hair. His father in Scotland had just written to say how proud he was of Dave for getting his para's wings. Months later, through the Legion grapevine, I heard that Dave was in Chad and had just been promoted to caporal.

Commenting on the future role of the Legion, Colonel Forcin—veteran of Vietnam and Algeria, and Second-in-Command of the Foreign Legion Group at Aubagne—saw his Legionnaires in the role of rapid deployment force, as they had been in Chad and Kolwezi, and of peacekeepers, as in Beirut. He maintained that there could always be found within the Legion a super-élite, able to carry out similar tasks to those of Britain's SAS.

Some observers—among them ex-Legionnaires—think that the Legion has been too slow in moving into the technological age, and that, as the latest weapons have been made available, there has been a shortage of trained manpower to operate them. The Legion, realizing that this could be a possible future weakness, aims to remedy the problem by intensifying the search for highly qualified candidates through its recruitment programme.

Commando training is designed to develop both teamwork and individual abilities. Selected Legionnaires are instructed in the use of a deadly weapon – the crossbow.

Like the Roman Legions before them, the French Foreign Legion provides builders as well as fighters. It is a proud claim of the Legion that, within its ranks, are men with every skill: architects and engineers, men who can construct barracks, schools and churches—even priests to serve the churches.

Sidi-bel-Abbès, that very heart of Legion history, was founded and built by Legionnaires. In French Guiana, Legion engineers and sappers are carving their way, with chain-saw and bulldozer, through the jungle, constructing the Route de l'Est, part of the Trans-American Highway system; while in southern France, they are building a military camp, roads and bridges.

The Legion as Builders

The Legion continues its long tradition of building and roadworks with important construction programmes. The picks and shovels of earlier generations have now been replaced by sophisticated tools and equipment.

83

Twentieth-Century Cavalry

The Foreign Legion's cavalry regiment (the 1st REC) is stationed at Orange. Like other mounted regiments in various parts of the world, it regards itself as being perhaps a little superior to its infantry brothers. Contrasting with other Legion regiments, the cavalry's chevrons, braid, and buttons are silver instead of gold, and its white wine is specially labelled with the regimental crest at the Legion's vineyards at Puyloubier. Although a small number of horses are kept for ceremonial purposes, it is the fast-moving light armoured vehicles (AMX 10-RC) that give the regiment its twentieth-century punch.

Like other modern cavalry regiments, the 1st REC's horses have given way to armoured vehicles.

The Sacred White Képi

For generations of Legionnaires, the white képi has been an object of near veneration. Around the world, in sand, swamps, and jungle, they have fought and died for it, representing, as it does, the honour of the Legion.

I had been invited to attend the ceremony of the *képi blanc*, which always takes place at sunset and by the light of flaming torches. As the ritual begins, the recruits hold behind their backs the white képi they are to wear for the first time. Torches are lit. The rows of young faces stare straight ahead. The commandant reminds them of their pledge of honour and fidelity. Together they sing *Le Boudin*, the song of the Legion, and place the white képi on their heads. It is a night they will remember for ever, for tonight they are truly Legionnaires.

The Legionnaire's most treasured possession is his white képi, which is presented to him at a ceremony some four weeks into his training. This takes place at dusk and is followed by a party and the singing of Legion songs around the camp fire.

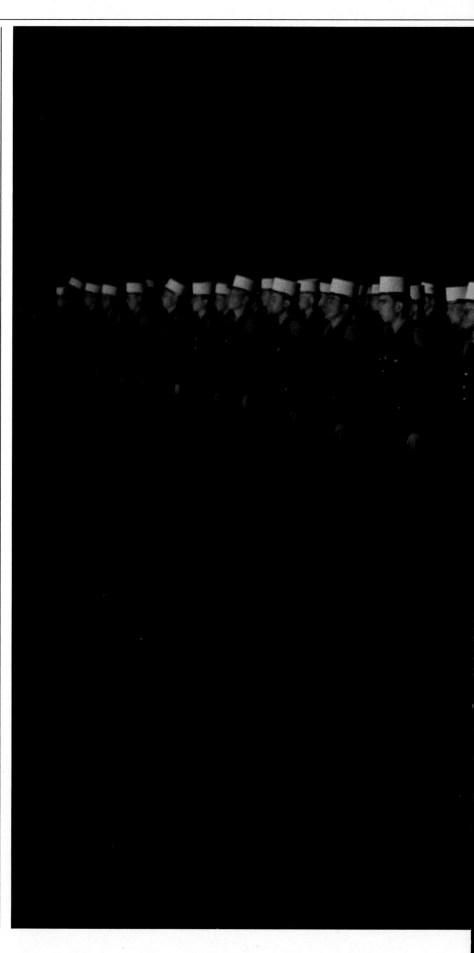

Commandos in Corsica: The Heroes of Kolwezi.

The 2nd REP on parade at Camp Raffalli, Calvi.

A little over half-an-hour's flying time from Nice, to the south of mainland France, lies the rugged holiday island of Corsica. In the summer months, its smooth white beaches and sandy coves are a mass of tourists from all parts of Europe. The local tourist office will remind the visitor that the island was the birthplace of Napoleon and that the small town of Calvi, in its northwest corner, was destroyed by Nelson in 1794. In recent years, Calvi has become famous for something else—the French Foreign Legion, as many a pretty girl will tell you. Some five miles outside Calvi, following the airport route, is Camp Raffalli, the headquarters of the Legion's élite airborne unit, the 2nd Foreign Parachute Regiment.

It was November. The air had a snap in it and condensed into small white puffs as you spoke. The first shafts of sunlight were hitting the nearby snow-covered mountain slopes as I slid into the parachute harness, assisted by a young British sergent. Expertly, he tightened the web harness over my shoulders and enquired if I was comfortable: 'Alright round your bum and crotch, Mr Young?' I doubted that he spoke so politely to his recruits. I felt like a trussed turkey, but refrained from saying so.

Once harnessed, the jump monitors moved us forward into the gaping rear of the Transall troop carrier, where we sat in two long rows in tip-up bucket seats along the length of the aircraft. There was light-hearted banter from a group on the starboard side. Apprehensively, some stared ahead, with their arms folded across their emergency 'chutes. The ramp at the rear of the Transall was raised and we taxied to the holding point, ready for take-off. The pilot released the brakes and the aircraft slowly gathered speed along the runway. Gently, the nose came up. A few seconds later, the undercarriage clunked into the fuselage. The flaps were raised, the throttles adjusted and the attitude trimmed for the climb to the jumping height.

The spectacular landscape of Corsica makes an ideal training ground. View over Camp Raffalli and Calvi from a mountain village.

The Green Beret and Winged Dagger

There is a definite air of swank tinged with arrogance about the Legionnaires of the 2nd REP. Their green berets, bearing the winged-hand-and-dagger emblem, are worn at a more rakish angle than in other regiments; képis are tipped a little more steeply over the eyes.

The basic parachute-training course at Calvi takes between three and four weeks, depending on the availability of aircraft for jumping. During the first week, the trainee is taken on several cross-country runs, the distance and speed increasing during the course of the week. This is followed by intensive training in safety and falling techniques. Then there is a final test. There are six jumps to be made from the Transall, one of them at night, before the Legionnaire will receive the coveted silver wings that he will wear on his right breast.

The Citadel of Calvi (opposite), *where officers of the 2nd REP have their mess. There they continue the Legion tradition of singing* Le Boudin *before meals. Tattooing is another old-established Legion tradition that is carried on by the younger Legionnaires. Members of the 2nd REP wear the silver emblem of the winged hand holding a dagger.*

There is no shortage of recruits for the 2nd REP, whose fame was established by its daring raid on Kolwezi in 1978.

'They Would Die for Me'

There is fierce competition within the Legion to serve with the 2nd REP, not only from non-commissioned ranks, but from officers also. One young officer put it this way: 'It gives you great satisfaction commanding a crack force. With conscripts, within a few months they are gone. They don't have the same dedication as my Legionnaires. I know my Legionnaires would die for me, and I for them.'

Legionnaires of the 2nd REP board a troop carrier for an early-morning drop.

The specialist Amphibious Section of the regiment trains along the waterways and rugged coastline of Corsica.

Ready for Instant Action

Possibly, few French taxpayers are aware that the Legion is kept in constant readiness for action, wherever events may require it.

On a wet November morning, the large troop-carrying helicopter edged its way on to the soggy landing zone behind Camp Raffalli. The sergent fired off a command and his Legionnaires dashed across the squelching sand to the waiting chopper. Crouching low under the slowly rotating blades, they scrambled into the dark interior. Here was one area of Legion training that had not changed radically since the Algerian campaign, when, operating with considerable success, Legionnaires were dropped by helicopter into areas of FLN terrorist activity.

While fulfilling their role as a rapid deployment force, Legionnaires of the 2nd REP, which has its own musicians, also enjoy the many attractions of life on Corsica. With their extra 'jump' pay, they can afford such luxuries as motor cycles.

In all seasons, the high ranges of Corsica form a natural training ground for the Legion's specialist Mountain Section.

They Dropped Like Ghosts

As the first shafts of morning sunlight struck the snow-covered mountain slopes, the Transall droned in from the sea. Inside, 'chutes were snapped on to the static line. Moments later, high above us, a trail of small black dots plummeted through the blue morning sky. Suddenly, the sky exploded with opening parachutes—ten, fifteen, twenty. The aircraft made a steep turn and headed back for more jumpers. The falling parachutists swayed, almost ghostlike, in the still morning air. Then came the sound of their voices as they called out to each other during the descent. Beside me, Capitaine Mole was not impressed. 'They should have jumped much tighter, so they would land closer together', he remarked. The remaining sticks of jumpers did make their exits much tighter. From the ground, it almost appeared as if they were ejected by some giant catapult. They were so close that there was a moment when they all appeared to be held together by a piece of string. After landing, they quickly packed their 'chutes and jogged to the camp.

It is six years since the 2nd REP made its daring raid on Kolwezi in Zaïre, to rescue families from the threat of massacre by Katangan rebels. At Kolwezi, the Legion's paratroops demonstrated that the intensive and sometimes ruthless training that they had undergone was more than justified. There must be few, in both military and civilian circles, who doubt the 'death or glory' mentality of these men. There are some who will point out that the interminable months of training for such units have only one purpose, and that is action. Yet action for the Legion is relatively thin on the ground these days. So the REP is concerned with a fresh dimension now and for the future. Its fighting pedigree is without question. It has survived in conflict. It remains to be seen if it can survive long periods of peace.

For those who wish to put their past life behind them, the Legion is a sanctuary. Others may rekindle old friendships in the outside world after serving out their contract. In a small graveyard near Calvi, some of the 2nd REP's dead are buried, their graves lovingly cared for by the Legion.

Before being awarded the silver wings of a parachutist, Legionnaires must make at least six jumps, one of them at night. Right: Returning to Camp Raffalli after an early-morning drop.

104

South American Jungle Patrol: Guyane.

In French Guiana's tropical rain forest.

Colonel Gosset looked at the blue tropical suit I was wearing and smiled. 'You will need some different clothes where you are going—we have some equipment for you in the stores.' The colonel commanded the 3rd Foreign Infantry Regiment in Guyane (French Guiana). He wore the scarlet ribbon of the Legion of Honour and his khaki drill shirt was sliced into the regulation pleats. Out of uniform, you might have thought he was an architect or doctor, with his sensitive face and gentle manner.

French Guiana is half a world away from the traditional home of the Foreign Legion—the desert and the Legionnaires' beloved Sidi-bel-Abbès. But it was to this overseas department of France in the jungles of South America that the 3rd REI was sent in 1973. In recent years, French Guiana has been used

for the firing of the European rocket Ariane, and a flurry of development has provided roads and port facilities to give easy access to the Space Centre at Kourou. It is here that the Legion has its headquarters in the Quartier Forget, a collection of modern buildings on the outskirts of the town.

Kourou has all the characteristics of many small French towns. A little bookshop sells *Marie Claire*, *L'Express* and *Elle*. Outside one of the cafés are the familiar red-and-blue umbrellas with 'Cinzano' printed over them. In the stifling heat and humidity of February, housewives and their daughters manage to stay cool and elegant—unmistakably French.

Only a few years ago, this was little more than a village of wooden and corrugated-iron huts, with a population of some six hundred. Locals scraped a living from fishing and a trickle of tourists. Now, an assortment of prefabricated houses, apartments and smart detached homes are all part of the new town.

The Legion's quartermaster's stores, with all the jungle equipment laid out on the wooden counter, rekindled memories of my service with the colonial police in Palestine. One of the sergents had already started packing the heavy-duty rucksack. Hammock, poncho, water bottle, jungle boots, combat boots, socks, and two sets of olive-green combat dress were signed for. A name tag with YOUNG, in large black letters, was to be worn above my left breast pocket.

The flight to Saint-Georges, from where we were to set out on a patrol up the Oyapock river bordering Brazil, took about forty-five minutes in the Transall troop carrier. Quickly, the local population became aware that the colonel was to inspect the Legion quarters at Camp Bernet, and the mayor came down to the local store to meet him. Equipment of all shapes and sizes, from generators to medical supplies, was unloaded by the Legionnaires on to the waiting trucks parked beside the runway. Soon they were speeding off to the Legion camp.

There was much to prepare before the dawn departure. In addition to each man's personal equipment, there were stores to gather, outboard engines to check, radios, life-jackets and gasoline to assemble. Everything would have to be manhandled on the patrol, except when carried in the pirogues—the local craft best suited to the shallows and rapids of the Oyapock. That night, I slept in the *sous-officiers'* dormitory, on a rickety iron cot and hard mattress, the cool air wafting through the wire gauze between the walls and the corrugated-iron roof.

To the uninitiated, pirogues look most unsafe. Sitting in the water, they resemble a long, slim tree-trunk with planks of wood tacked on to the sides. The Legion employs its own piroguiers, Creole boatmen who have a natural affinity with the river. Two piroguiers, one handling the powerful outboard engine, the other in the bows, navigate these craft along hundreds of miles of local rivers.

As the soft rim of morning light slid over the palm trees, a small band of villagers had gathered to see our departure. The Legionnaires chatted amongst themselves in a mixture of French, German and English. There were several English-speaking men in the section, with accents that echoed Sydney, the Mersey and Bengal. Who were these Legionnaires and what had brought them here? Ranji Singh, I discover, is a caporal-chef who has nine years' service in the Legion. His family in India is certainly not without money; he has had a good education and appears to have left his country for political reasons. At home, he was at university and training to be a pharmacist, which made him the obvious choice for medical orderly. Ranji Singh told me of his plans for the future. 'The Legion has been good to me. Like all military organizations, you have to do as you are told; the Legion is stricter than most armies.' He smiled. 'That is, except for your British army, which we regard highly in India. If you do as you are told, and do it well, you can have a good life in the Legion. I will stay on long enough to qualify for a small pension; then I would like to return to France, study for a profession, and marry. But right now, the Legion is my home and family.'

It is interesting to observe how each Legionnaire expresses his personality through his hat. Brims are bent and twisted into a multitude of shapes that would suit no one but the owner. One of the sergents wears his in strict regimental fashion, the brim as though neatly pressed. King and his companion Heinz tie the wide brims up, Western-style. The lieutenant has curled his brim, but not to excess. Occasionally, he props it forward over his eyes, to give him more protection from the sun.

The jungle is so dense that you can only see a few yards into the forest as you pass close to the shore. Lieutenant Gravereau taps me on the shoulder and passes his water bottle. 'Drink, Monsieur Young. There are tablets in the water to stop you sweating too much.' The liquid is surprisingly cool and tastes of bitter lemon. It is certainly refreshing.

There is no warning. A strong current grips the pirogue and we are hit by the white water. The torrent swooshes in over the bows and sides. Our two Creoles are shouting instructions to each other, as the boat flays its way helplessly on to the rocks. The boatman in the bows attempts to fend us off with his long pole. It snaps, and the pirogue gives another lurch. The outboard engine screams as the propeller spins clear of the water. The boatman heaves it back and twists the handle to full power. The engine is losing the battle against the current, and more water pours over the sides of the boat. The three other pirogues are now in similar trouble, each fighting its battle against the river. Above the noise, an Australian voice shouts, 'Not that way, you stupid bastard! You'll get us all killed!' The engine fails to move us against the swift current, and Lieutenant Gravereau

The River Oyapock, route to the interior.

is over the side with four Legionnaires, heaving the boat up the rapids. King grabs Dallon, a young Belgian, who has lost his grip, and drags him back. He surfaces, spitting out mouthfuls of water and gasping for air. The pirogue takes in more water and threatens to break loose. With a rope secured to the bows, Gravereau urges his men on, and those on shore start hauling. Then, as suddenly as it started, the danger is over.

Some days later, the lieutenant walked with me to the small Britten-Norman Islander aircraft loading passengers on the dirt airstrip at Saint-Georges. We grasped each other's arms and said farewell like old comrades. As the plane turned on course for Kourou, I looked back through the windows on the starboard side and saw the winding silver thread of the Oyapock. For the Legionnaires of the 2nd Company stationed at Saint-Georges, another mission had been completed without incident.

To meet the changing needs of its time, the Legion has proved that it can always adapt. Legionnaires today have reconciled themselves to the jungles of Guiana as readily as their brothers before them did to the rice fields of Indo-China.

The Saint-Georges Detachment

Camp Caporal Bernet is situated on a gentle slope near the dirt runway on which we had just landed, ten minutes' stroll from the town of Saint-Georges. Like military camps the world over, it has a liberal sprinkling of whitewash on stones and walls. A gentle breeze stirs the tricolour on the camp flagpole, and small lizards scurry for the nearest shade.

This is open-plan living. The sleeping quarters are divided between *sous-officiers* and légionnaires, while the mess provides excellent food and wine in an atmosphere of friendly informality. A lieutenant, with his senior NCOs, commands the thirty-man detachment, which is rotated every two months.

At the colonel's approach, the Legionnaires, drawn up in neat straight lines outside their living quarters, smack their FA MAS rifles smartly in salute. They wear well-pressed khaki shorts, Ranger boots, green berets and combat jackets. Many of the faces betray their nationality: Slav, Latin, African and Anglo-Saxon. The colonel speaks slowly, in clear, simple French that all can understand. He is satisfied with the smartness of the section and their quarters, and wishes them well on the forthcoming patrol. They salute again briskly, with a crack of the hand on the rifle, and return to their barracks.

At Saint-Georges, the starting point for patrols along the Oyapock, Legionnaires of the 3rd REI enjoy a meal in their mess, a short march from Camp Bernet. Local people are employed to prepare the food.

The Village Store

It was time for an aperitif, and the Legion stopped for refreshment at what might have been the edge of the world. As the colonel had said, it was not Maxim's; the bar was a wooden store in the square next to the town hall. Like all such stores in remote corners of the earth, it sold everything. The shelves were lined with tins of corned beef from the Argentine, beans from Britain and olives from Italy. The small glass cabinet on the counter held buttons, mingled with batteries and hairgrips, but the large madame who served, along with several children, seemed to know where to find everything.

There was no shortage of drinks. The best Scotch, gin, brandy, Cinzano and a multitude of other coloured bottles lined the shelves, just as in any café from Dieppe to Marseilles. Inside the store, Legionnaires guzzled cold beer from cans beneath an ageing picture of the long-departed President de Gaulle.

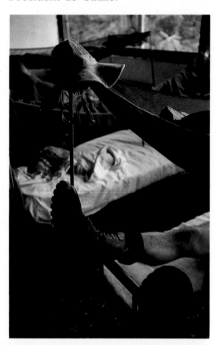

Legionnaires are posted for several weeks at a time to Saint-Georges from their headquarters at Kourou, to undertake missions into the jungle. Saint-Georges has one main store, which supplies everything from razor blades to beer. Across the square, the men can pass their time playing billiards and drinking at the small bar.

Chess is a popular pastime in the austere barracks at Saint-Georges.

Danger is always present for the Legion patrols that navigate the Oyapock in narrow pirogues, driven by powerful outboard motors.

Bypassing the Rapids

At Saut Maripa, some ten miles up-river from Saint-Georges, everything has to be manhandled through the jungle for a mile or two on a narrow railway, in order to bypass the rapids. A truck, the size of a scout handcart, is pushed on to the rails and loaded with equipment.

Lunch is eaten on a small island of rock and sand in a quiet stretch of water above the rapids. The hot sun quickly dries out the wet pirogues and clothing. There is little conversation as the Legionnaires unpack their rations and spread themselves out along the sand. Lieutenant Gravereau finds a quiet corner, lies down and takes out a fresh packet of Gauloises. King and his two companions, Heinz and Dallon, open their tins of sardines.

Even on patrol, high standards of appearance and hygiene are maintained. Food may be packaged rations or wild game, while heavy equipment must often be manhandled through the jungle. Overleaf: A smooth stretch of the Oyapock.

The light was softening and the shadows cobalt blue when the four pirogues cut their engines and drifted on to the flat rocks beside the campsite. Within half an hour, everyone had erected his shelter. The quietness of the forest was uncanny, its vastness dampening voices to a soft whisper. The only sound was the rhythmic beep of the radio signals reaching the two operators a few yards away.

A musty, dank smell hung around the forest. 'You've got to find trees further apart than that, Mr Young.' It was the Englishman, King, stripped to the waist and wanting to help. 'Bloody stores haven't given you all the kit you need for this lark.' He had already started unravelling the mass of cord that was part of my hammock, when Heinz came to help him. 'Don't forget to take a sweater or something to wrap up in when you turn in tonight. It's OK now, but it'll freeze the balls off you later.' The air was still warm, and flies skipped across the water as several of us swam and splashed about in the river. It felt good to be rid of the day's sweat and to float on one's back looking up at the Southern Cross. And then there was the evening meal to look forward to, cooking on a wood fire while one of the sergents gave it an occasional stir with a stick.

The Jungle Bivouac

First aid is applied from the comprehensive medical supplies carried on every jungle patrol. Vitamin and anti-malaria tablets are issued daily.

After preparing the night's bivouac, Legionnaires line up for the evening meal.

In the Depths of the Rain Forest

At least once a year, Legionnaires in French Guiana go on a jungle patrol for up to forty-five days. The *mission profonde*, they call it, when personal training and fitness are pushed to the limit and beyond, with the men carrying heavy loads of equipment through the fiercest jungles in the world. Slashing a path through these dense forests, patrols may cover only four or five miles in a day, hacking every yard of the way with a machete. A caporal said that it was the constant wetness of everything that annoyed him. Day after day, nothing was dry; what with sweat and rain, always one's clothes were wet.

Before going out on long patrols into the jungle, Legionnaires posted to French Guiana are sent to a jungle-training school close to Kourou. Here they learn the art of survival in their unfamiliar and potentially hostile new surroundings.

An Oyampi Indian Village

Lieutenant Gravereau was to make a routine visit to the Oyampi Indian village at Camopi, about four hours upstream from the campsite. We travelled light, with only the rations for the day and fuel for the outboard engine.

The village is one of the largest Oyampi communities in the area, with a dispensary, gendarmerie, radio station, and sufficient open space to land a helicopter. A group of Indians

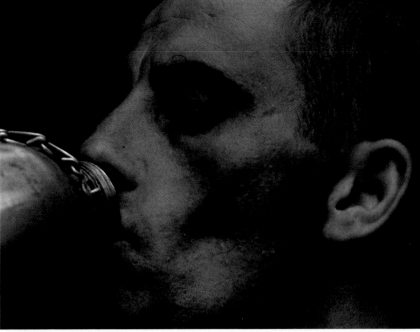

watched our arrival from the bank. The Oyampis are a handsome people; their lithe chestnut-brown bodies and ochre-red loincloths contrasted with the brilliant green of the forest. Some carried small bows and arrows, others long spears, both of which they use with great skill for fishing.

Chickens scattered as we ducked under a low thatched roof to speak with some of the villagers. The Oyampis use simple French, although an outsider still finds this difficult to understand. Two of the Legionnaires began to bargain for chickens, which would make a pleasant change from

the wild pig that we had eaten the previous evening.

We wandered through the village for about an hour, visiting families in their huts. Finally, after shaking hands with the village chief, we made our way back to the boat, with some of the children following.

Camopi, an Oyampi Indian village several days up-river from Saint-Georges, is visited by Legionnaires of the 3rd REI on patrol along the Brazilian border.

122

Return to Africa: Djibouti and the Desert.

The 13th DBLE on desert patrol.

Travel always has its hazards, regardless of the century or the place, and there are few journeys where the traveller does not arrive at his destination without a mixture of relief and exasperation. Landing in Djibouti at three in the morning, along with several hundred other passengers on the Air France 747 from Paris, is not the happiest of introductions to the country. As we crowded into the small airport terminal, children wailed from lack of sleep and families reached out to greet their loved ones. Immigration officers took their time, methodically checking that all residents' papers were in order, or that temporary visitors had a valid return ticket.

The scramble for the luggage had begun. Pulling and grabbing, everyone was involved in the final struggle before rejoining family or friends and going home. As the last few bags arrived from the plane, I sensed trouble. The carton containing the film stock was not among them.

Commandant Dufour was waiting for me at the exit gate, together with his spaniel puppy. He must have been in his mid-thirties, with the build of a well-seasoned tennis player. It was a relief to hear his excellent flow of English, for at this early hour my French was decidedly poor. He was not surprised to learn about the lost film. *'C'est l'Afrique'*, he smiled whimsically. 'Don't worry. I'm sure we can solve the problem tomorrow.'

The Quartier Gabode, home of the Foreign Legion's 13th Half-Brigade, which fought at Bir Hakeim, El Alamein, Dien Bien Phu and in Algeria, is situated some ten minutes from the centre of Djibouti and only a short distance from the airport. I was pleased to find myself assigned to a modest air-conditioned room in the officers' quarters. I was the sole occupant of the twin-bedded accommodation which had been prepared for me. A simple white sheet covered the bed, together with a pillow and the traditional military blanket. A large picnic cooler stood in one corner and, peering inside, I discovered that it was stocked with beer, Perrier water and a selection of cold drinks surrounded by ice. Switching off the noisy air conditioner, I turned on the old fan in the centre of the ceiling, which had seen better days. Within minutes, I was asleep.

By mid-morning, I was awake and splashing around in the shower room close by. As I was leaving, a jeep drew up alongside and a sergent called me. 'Monsieur Young. Bonjour. I have a message for you.' He handed me a carefully written note from Commandant Dufour: 'Just let the Sergeant know how many rolls of colour film you require. I have located some with the Marine [French Navy]. You are to lunch with the Colonel in the Officers' Mess at 12.00.' I was relieved to know that some film had been found for me, and I asked the sergent to bring sixty rolls.

Djibouti, once known as French Somaliland, is situated at the southern entrance to the Red Sea in that smouldering area of confrontation, the Horn of Africa. It is among the smallest countries in the world, being roughly a hundred miles from north to south and ninety-five from east to west. Apart from a small area on the southeast border which gives access to Somalia, Djibouti is surrounded by Ethiopia. Like so many other parts of Africa, the country suffers from poverty and the problems of refugees. The refugees pour across her borders, fleeing the ravages of drought, famine and Ethiopia's conflicts with Somalia and Eritrea. Ten years ago, Djibouti had a population of a little under 100,000. Today, it is nearer a quarter of a million, the majority of them living in shanty towns on the outskirts of the city of Djibouti. The republic became independent in 1977, but still relies heavily on France, especially for her defence. As one member of the English-speaking community said to me during my visit, 'It is a great relief to know that the Foreign Legion are just down the road.'

Boredom has always been a problem with Legionnaires, especially in remote postings. In contrast with the Legion's early years in Morocco and Algeria, where small detachments could be posted to desert forts for months at a time, and where the relief unit could arrive weeks late, today's Legionnaires have an easy time. Veterans returning to visit their old units told me that sports facilities were rare in their day. A few jugs of beer or red wine, and a visit to the local bordello, were the extent of their recreation.

Moucha is one of a small group of tiny islands just off the coast in the Gulf of Aden. It is about twenty minutes away in a bouncing rubber Zodiac, powered by a sixty-horsepower outboard motor, and is frequently used by the 13th DBLE as a rest and recreation area. Some of them were there now and

had invited me to join them. It was a lovely day, with a few clouds breaking the fierce sun, and refreshing to be away from the humid nineties of the mainland. There were about twenty Legionnaires scattered around a little sandy cove, wearing an assortment of coloured swimming trunks, floppy hats and shirts. A couple of them were fishing from the ruined jetty. They put down their rods and gave me a strong heave out of the lurching Zodiac. Grabbing my camera bag, they ushered me along the jetty to the shelter of their campsite—an open-air construction with asbestos roof, which gave welcome protection against the midday sun. Nearby was one of the island's navigation lights, surrounded by ruined outbuildings, which was now used as an observation tower by visitors. In charge of the party was a hefty adjudant with a rippling girth that had leant against many a Legion bar. Seated on crates of beer, four men were playing cards on an ancient wooden camp table, while their companions prepared the salad and steak for lunch. A couple of brown bodies snoozed away on their sleeping bags spread out on the sand. With a practised hand, the adjudant snapped the metal cap from a bottle of Kronenberg lager and gave it to me. The cool liquid helped take away the salt taste that the Zodiac journey had left in my mouth.

It was obvious that being away from the normal strict military life of the Quartier Gabode was a welcome relief to these men. There was no discipline as such. Each did what he wished to do: fish, swim, read or lie in the sun. They still called each other by their rank—Adjudant, Chef or Sergent—but the tone was softer. Making the lunch was no labour for the little team in the corner that was perfecting each dish with the care of chefs laying on a banquet at the George V in Paris. It was a holiday for all of them—a grand family outing—and they could do what they liked for a few days. For most of them, this was the only family they had.

Two Legionnaires are promoted by their commanding officer at a remote outstation.

A Voice Like Piaf

Lunch was delicious. A freshly caught fish was shared amongst half a dozen of us, and was washed down by liberal helpings of red wine. It had been cooked in the embers of a wood fire and it melted in the mouth. The meal continued late into the afternoon. This was the men's last day on Moucha and there was still plenty of wine and beer to drink. It was after the sergent had been sprayed with Perrier water that they all shouted for Michael to sing. 'He is fantastic, Monsieur Young', said the caporal next to me. 'He sings like Piaf.'

Michael was skinny as a jackrabbit. His ears protruded slightly and there were three or four teeth missing from the right-hand side of his mouth. The notes quivered as he sang the haunting melody of *L'Etranger*, his body swaying and his hands stretched out to his audience. It was uncanny, for he did sing just like Piaf. Along with Michael's repertoire of songs went a selection of quick-fire jokes, aimed at the adjudant and sergent, which brought howls of laughter from his comrades.

Rest and recreation periods are arranged for Legionnaires following long patrols and outstation postings. Overleaf: *Helicopter patrol over Lake Assal, a salt-encrusted lake below sea level.*

126

Towards the Desert Interior

The rotor blades of the Alouette four-seater helicopter sliced the air with a high-pitched whine as we lifted off from the French Air Force base just outside Djibouti. I had been issued with two emergency water bottles, which were threaded on to my web belt, since we would be flying over remote areas of desert. The doors had been removed from each side of the helicopter, to allow us as much cool air as possible and to give maximum visibility for photography. Leaving the coast behind us, the pilot set a southwesterly course for Hol-Hol and Dikhil, where he would turn north towards the Ethiopian border for our refuelling stop at Yoboki.

Lake Assal, thirty minutes' flying time east of Djibouti. The area provides excellent training facilities, including a Commando Training Centre at Arta Plage.

Patrolling the Hostile Wastes

The helicopter skimmed so close to the ground that I felt as if I were on a flying carpet. The reddish-brown, flat landscape was desolate and lonely. We crossed the single-track railway leading to Addis Ababa and a collection of mud and timber houses, together with their precious goats and camels. Now the colours had changed to varying shades of green and purple and the ground rose steeply on either side. I could have almost reached out and touched the rocks. Then up and over we soared, like a giant condor, to look down on a sight of savage beauty. The desert seemed to reach beyond the horizon, and the distant mountains shimmered in the scalding heat below. Nothing moved. There was no life, no trees or rocks; just endless rippling sand. I pondered on being stranded in such a hostile environment, for this is where the Legion carries out its regular desert patrols. Lost in this heat, a man would have little chance of survival.

Desert patrols of the 13th DBLE are equipped with 7.5 mm. light machine guns (left), while Legionnaires carry one of the latest personal weapons – the 5.56 mm. FA MAS. The marksman (above) is using a 7.5 mm. rifle with telescopic sight.

A Reconnaissance Squadron crossing a desert area near its base at Weah, south of the Gulf of Tadjoura.

A Night Beneath the Stars

In a bivouac at the edge of the desert, I slept under the stars, along with a twenty-man patrol of the 13th DBLE's Reconnaissance Squadron. I had returned with the helicopter to Djibouti, and had then travelled north-west by jeep, over rough mountain roads, to reach the campsite between Lake Assal and the coast.

As night was falling, a young man walked towards me out of the shadows, a slight nervousness in his manner. He gave his name as Martin Darcy and said he was nineteen. The soft lilt of his voice told me he was Irish. Had the training at Castelnaudary been tough on him? I asked. Like all the Irish when telling a story, he philosophized a little: 'It affects people in different ways. Yes, there were times when it was rough, but I survived.'

The intense heat and humidity of Djibouti make frequent laundering essential. Boot cleaning and shaving are part of a patrol's regular morning routine.

Reveille before Sunrise

The previous evening's meal had been eaten in the *sous-officiers'* mess, under a thorn tree, with Lieutenant Dury at the head of the table. There had been the usual military banter, and plans had been made for the following day. Now, with the first glimmer of light, the morning routine began.

Some shaved in a truck mirror, while others hung their camp mirrors in the branches of thorn trees. Coffee was slurped and bread and jam gulped down; boots were brushed, tunics made as smart as possible, and green berets adjusted to the usual rakish angle for the morning parade. Surely, there couldn't be many parades like this taking place around the world.

In a small clearing surrounded by desert scrub, the sergent-chef brought the Legionnaires to attention. He turned and saluted the lieutenant, and reported that his men were ready for duty. Another day in the Legion had begun.

The day starts before sunrise for a desert patrol of the 13th DBLE. Breakfast is hot black coffee, bread and jam.

Dawn parade at the edge of the desert for men of the 13th DBLE.

The Legion Is My Family: The Ties of Comradeship.

The Legion is a large and diverse family.

The French Foreign Legion is far more than simply a sanctuary and refuge for men who have abandoned their past and seek to escape to a new life. It is a 'family'. A family, like all families, that will care for its members until they die. There are times when this brotherhood of Legionnaires rivals any city 'old boy' network or secret society. There is a bond of fellowship which develops between officers and other ranks which any military force would envy. I have even heard senior officers refer to légionnaires as their 'sons'. Colonel Bertrand de La Presle, who commanded the 1st Foreign Cavalry Regiment until September 1983, expressed his feelings this way: 'These Legionnaires are, for us, another family, and not just soldiers we have to form and train.' The family is composed of many races and creeds—Germans, Britons, Greeks and Africans; Jews, Catholics, Muslims and Buddhists—yet all are Legionnaires.

You turn right, a hundred yards or so before coming to the centre of Puyloubier, to reach the home of the old Legionnaires. A battered signpost points the way along a narrow, bumpy road that allows a generous view of the rolling countryside across the vineyards. Go through the wrought-iron gates at the end of the road and you are in the courtyard of the Domaine Capitaine Danjou. It was during a visit there that I met one of the Legion's more venerable characters—a Russian-born cavalry officer, Capitaine Solomirsky. After the Bolshevik Revolution, many White Russians fled to France and later became the nucleus of the Legion's own cavalry regiment, the 1st REC. It is said that the capitaine was once a page-boy in the Court of the Tsars. His eighty-year-old waxlike face, with its silver hair and glittering eyes, still retains something of a cherubic appearance. He lives in a small house close to the bookbinding shop. At mealtimes in the refectory, he may sit in a corner and eat alone, or at times be joined by a few old friends he has known over the years. Veterans will tell you that old Solomirsky led one of the Legion's last cavalry charges, during his service in North Africa (see the painting on page 30). To see him walking along the lanes around Puyloubier, hair and cloak flying in the breeze, it is not difficult to imagine him leading the charge under a scorching Moroccan sky. You could not but wonder how he felt now, as he reconciled himself to the cradle of the Legion after so many years of command.

It is 29 April, the eve of Camerone. The air is clear and fresh and the sky a rich blue. The noonday sun is now warm enough to pierce the cool shadows under the trees. A gentle breeze wafts down the nearby mountains. At the little Puyloubier cemetery, a few minutes' walk from the veterans' home, a handful of German old comrades and their families gather to remember those who died in the rice paddies and the sand. '*Eins, zwei, eins, zwei*', a tall, middle-aged veteran quietly calls out the time to the small group bearing its flags and floral tribute. They proudly wear their green berets, each with its Legion emblem. On their dark-blue blazers, medals glint in the sunlight. Following behind are wives, sons and daughters, carrying cameras and flowers. Few speak. The only sound is the crunch of marching feet on the cemetery gravel. Beside the graves of General Rollet, Prince Aage of Denmark and Légionnaire Zimmermann, the flags are dipped. In this quiet country graveyard in southern France, looking out towards the distant mountains, the Legion family remembers its dead.

Arthur De Silva is in his early thirties and is one of the Legion's bright young men. After ten years' service, he is a sergent-chef. It is only a matter of time before he is promoted to adjudant, and he has every intention of applying for officer training. He lives with his wife Marie and two young sons, David and Segerick, in the Legion's married quarters, close to the Quartier Viénot. Surrounded by trees and overlooking Aubagne, the married quarters are a cluster of modern apartment blocks, of the kind frequently seen on the outskirts of many French towns. The two-bedroomed apartment, one of fifteen in the block, is rented by the De Silvas for a little over a thousand francs a month. The rent is lower than the normal rate for the area, as it is subsidized by the Legion. The De Silvas also receive a marriage allowance in their monthly pay-cheque of some eight thousand francs. David and Segerick attend school in Aubagne, and every morning, together with other children from the Quartier, are taken there by the Legion's school bus. When the time comes for an overseas posting, like other military organizations, the Legion will store the family's furniture, unless they wish to sell it and start afresh when they return.

I vividly recall being driven up the autoroute from Marseilles to Orange at Christmas in a swish black Alfa Romeo. It belonged to the sergent-chef who had been sent by the Colonel of the 1st REC to collect me. He could have been Belgian or Dutch, and he spoke excellent English. 'The parties started two or three days ago and everyone is pretty merry back at the barracks', he told me. 'You are expected at 1.00 p.m. in the brigadier-chefs' mess, as soon as we arrive. *Marraine* arrived a few days ago and has already given several parties.' The Comtesse Ladis-las du Luart is a Commander of the National Order of the Legion of Honour. She is also an Officer of the Order of Merit and holds the Croix de Guerre and the Croix de Valeur Militaire. She is one of the great personalities of the French Foreign Legion, and especially of the 1st Foreign Cavalry. To them she is *Marraine*—Godmother. She is one of the few women ever to hold an honorary rank within the Legion, having been made an honorary brigadier-chef in 1944 for her patronage and devoted service with the regiment.

It must have been about three in the morning as I made my way to the waiting jeep parked under the trees near the regimental offices. The clear night air was bitterly cold. Perhaps there would be snow before morning. As we drove through the gates into the deserted boulevard, the muffled harmony of the Legionnaires' singing—'*Stille Nacht, Heilige Nacht*'—drifted through the barracks. I shook hands with the two Legionnaires who had accompanied me and fumbled for the key to the hotel door. '*Bonne nuit, Monsieur Young. Joyeux Noël.*' '*Joyeux Noël*', I replied, and closed the door behind me.

The ancient jeep roared through the narrow alleys into the main street and disappeared from view. I had spent Christmas in many corners of the world, from Canada to Africa and Israel. But Christmas within the family of the Legion was one I would always remember.

Capitaine Solomirsky (on the right) *joined the Legion from Russia after the Revolution.*

Families within the Family

The De Silva home is bright and spotlessly clean, with modern furniture and neat lace curtains at the windows. Over an aperitif, the family chatted to me about married life in the Legion. 'I have to get used to being on my own a great deal, as my husband could be away for long periods on courses or training exercises', said Madame De Silva. 'I realized when I married a Legionnaire that his first obligation would be to the Legion. But being a Legion wife has more advantages than disadvantages. There are opportunities for us to travel and see other countries; more so than many civilians.'

Legion families are a close-knit community and wives understand that there are times when the Legion comes first. After the initial five-year contract, a Legionnaire may obtain permission to marry.

Comfortable houses or apartments are available for all married officers and men. A family allowance is paid, and rents are modest. Family functions are arranged to maintain the spirit of the Legion or of the regiment.

Love, Marriage and the Legion

Broadly speaking, most well-brought-up French women have mixed feelings about Legionnaires—that is, apart from those who have married into the Legion. This coolness is frequently coloured by the odd bar-room brawl, which can take place in any garrison town, be it Aldershot or Calvi. However, there can be no doubt that, for some women, there is a touch of magic about the white képi and the men who wear it. As any member of the 2nd REP will tell you, during the summer months the beaches of Calvi are awash with the most attractive girls from all corners of Europe, searching for a Legion lover to share their annual holiday.

In affairs of the heart, the Legion is both tolerant and open-minded, compared, say, to a British Guards Regiment. It is not unknown for Legionnaires to marry girls from exotic ethnic backgrounds. Once married, they are looked upon with respect by general and légionnaire alike, as they are now members of the 'family'. On the other hand, should it be thought, for whatever reason, that an intended marriage was not in the best interests of the Legion, that marriage would be discouraged.

Female company and an intimate candlelit dinner make a pleasant change from the Legion mess and the rigours of training.

The Puyloubier Pilgrimage

A lone bugler plays the haunting notes of the Last Post. There is a single wreath, from the Old Comrades' Association in Hamburg and Schleswig-Holstein, of white lilies and red roses, surrounded by evergreen. Attached is a green-and-red ribbon, bearing the simple message in Gothic script: 'To our Comrades'. The wreath is placed against the grey stone memorial. For a while, the pilgrims stand, silently remembering those whose names are carved in stone.

In the small cemetery at Puyloubier, old comrades and their families visit the Legion's memorial. Legionnaires from all parts of the world make the pilgrimage to honour their dead.

Veterans of the Indo-China and Algerian campaigns, along with other old comrades, are cared for by the Legion at the Domaine Danjou, near Puyloubier. At the veterans' home, many old Legionnaires are engaged in woodwork, ceramics and bookbinding.

The Legion Cares for Its Own

A dozen or so miles to the west of the little town of Saint Maximin in southern France, to the north of the A 7, lies the village of Puyloubier. Here also is the Domaine Capitaine Danjou, home for some 180 veteran Legionnaires, who will live out the remainder of their days in peace, cared for by the Legion.

They are an active lot, these Legion pensioners, many of them still eager to enjoy a full day's labour in the vineyards, or to turn their hand to small craft industries. Some make furniture. Others become potters, producing beer mugs, ash trays and various other souvenirs for the Legion's gift shops. There is also a small bookbinding department, where, under the supervision of a master-craftsman, once a member of the French Resistance, the old soldiers are taught the delicate art of binding and embossing.

But there are some who will never work again, crippled by wounds sustained on the battlefields of Indo-China, Morocco or Algeria. Skilled medical staff look after them, totally dedicated to the care of these old campaigners. Some sit in wheelchairs outside their rooms, gazing out over the soft, rolling landscape; others still maintain that disciplined bearing that is the hallmark of all 'old soldiers'.

Legion shops sell a range of souvenirs made by the veterans, both to visitors and to Legion families. For many, it is the wines from the Legion's vineyards that are the principal attraction. Much of the wine is consumed in the Legion's own messes.

Camerone: The Family Celebrates

As April approaches, Legionnaires will say on parting, *'Au revoir. A Camerone.'* Every year, wherever they are, the Legion and its old comrades meet to commemorate the battle fought at a lonely farmhouse in Mexico more than a century ago.

It is during this yearly act of remembrance that, at Aubagne, the wooden hand of Capitaine Danjou, in its glass casket, is paraded before the Legion. The presentation of the hand symbolizes the spirit of the Legion's brotherhood. They come to Aubagne each year from all parts of the world, these ex-Legionnaires and their families. For them it is a pilgrimage. In returning to their 'Mother House' in Provence, Legionnaires relive their glorious past.

After the parade, it is party time for the Legion. Wives, sons, daughters and girlfriends mingle with the 'old sweats' from Algeria and Indo-China—general and légionnaire alike. They drink Legion wine from the vineyards of Puyloubier, sing Legion songs, consume plates of salad, garlic-sausage and ham. Children lick chocolate ice-cream, drink fizzy lemonade, play games of chance, and throw fluffy balls at rows of tins. The 'family' is having a giant picnic.

Camerone Day is not only for the Legion and its veterans, but also for wives, families and sweethearts, who attend the two days of celebrations. At Aubagne, the grounds take on a carnival air, to the great delight of the children, while other visitors study the unique historical collections in the Legion's museum.

The Monthly Pay Day

During their early years in the Legion, the men rarely have bank accounts. There is a military banking system, which many use to deposit a proportion of their pay.

In his first few months of service, a recruit will receive a little less than 1700 francs a month. After three years, if he has not been posted overseas, his pay will have increased by some four hundred francs to 2091 francs a month. He would be paid much more if he managed to gain a posting to the 2nd REP, the para regiment, where he would receive 3115 francs. The extra money is 'jump' pay.

Overseas service can, in some circumstances, more than double a man's pay. In Djibouti, for example, a légionnaire with less than a year's service will be paid a little over 5000 francs a month.

Legionnaires qualify for a small pension after fifteen years' service. However, many reengage to earn the better pension that comes after twenty years in the Legion.

After saluting smartly and giving his name, rank and length of service, the Legionnaire presents his identity card. Then, with a sweep of the hand, he collects his pay in his white képi.

Christmas Eve at Orange

When Legionnaires sing, there is passion in their voices. You cannot help but be stirred by it. Even the most hardened campaigner feels the hair rise at the back of his neck. The harmony has a blend of the Welsh valleys and the Russian steppes in it, and a resonance all its own. As the Legion sings, its history unfolds.

It is Christmas. A small choir of Legionnaires quietly sings carols in one of the tank hangers at the Quartier Labouche in Orange. This is the headquarters of the Legion's cavalry regiment, the 1st REC, with whom I had been invited to spend Christmas. The cavelike interior glows a bluey-green from the overhead lighting. An altar has been erected for the midnight Mass. In a corner, the Legion's own priest pulls the vestments over his head and intones the preparatory prayers with the Legionnaires who will assist him in the service.

Celebrating Christmas is something very special for Legionnaires. Few of them have homes to go to, unless they are married. The Legion is their home and the bonds of its own 'family' are tight. So much so that, traditionally, during Christmas, all officers and *sous-officiers* remain with their men until after the *réveillon*, the Christmas Eve vigil and feast, is over. Wives and sweethearts understand and accept this custom as a normal part of sharing their lives with a Legionnaire.

Christmas. The Legion 'family' gathers to celebrate one of the most important feasts of the year. Many Legionnaires attend the midnight Mass, which is followed by Christmas dinner. Wives and families do not attend the dinner.

The Cavalry's 'Godmother'

'*Marraine*' enters the mess, escorted by the colonel, and the fifty or so occupants stand to attention. She is a handsome woman, the Comtesse Ladislas du Luart. Only the fine lines around her pale face betray her seventy or more years. You cannot mistake the distinct military bearing, and yet she radiates a simple motherly quality as she moves around the room. Every man present receives a light kiss on each cheek. These are her 'boys', her Legionnaires. The mess presents its Christmas gifts to 'Godmother' and the colonel. As her slender, well-manicured hands unwrap the crinkly paper, her eyes sparkle with delight. She peers into the dainty box, pauses, and after a few moments, with a girlish merriment in her voice, thanks them.

After the midnight Mass, the Christmas merrymaking continued until dawn. During the evening, every Legionnaire received a carefully gift-wrapped present, which he himself had chosen, from his company commander—radios, watches, toilet sets. Christmas dinner was poultry, with lashings of red wine and cheese.

The Comtesse Ladislas du Luart, 'Godmother' of the 1st REC and honorary brigadier-chef, is guest of honour at the Christmas celebrations. During Christmas week, Legionnaires show great ingenuity constructing and animating cribs of the Nativity in their barracks.

Opposite: *It is a tradition of the Legion that each Legionnaire receives a Christmas gift of his choice, which is presented to him by his company commander.*

Honneur et Fidélité: Pride, Tradition and Mystique.

A Legion veteran's campaign medals.

Were it not for the sentry in sparkling white képi, red epaulettes and blue waist sash, passing through the gates of the Quartier Viénot at Aubagne would not be unlike entering any other military establishment. The Chef de Poste recognizes the French car with the British number plates, smiles and waves me through. The parade ground is larger than that at Sidi-bel-Abbès. The hard lines of buildings are softened by shrubs and trees. Snuggling under the distant mountain range, there is the suggestion of an American university campus about it. Passing one of the buildings overlooking the square, the visitor may well hear the clatter of a modern printing press, mixed with the pungent aroma of inks. These are the offices and printing works of the Legion's own monthly magazine, *Képi Blanc*. With a circulation of several thousand, it is a highly professional journal, containing racy colour features, competitions, reports from the

regiments, crosswords and cartoons. Looking every bit the image of the executive journalist is its editor, Commandant Chiaroni. A dapper figure, he can be seen at all hours peering over the light box at a set of transparencies from Beirut or Chad, or briefing technicians in the machine room.

A muted trumpet, coupled with the swinging trill of a clarinet, echoes from a small building, partly hidden by trees, at the end of the road. These are the quarters of the ninety-strong Legion band. Its unique musical style attracts huge crowds whenever it plays at military and public gatherings. The band features two of the world's oldest instruments, the fife and drum, as well as that unusual form of percussion, the 'Chinese pavilion' or 'jingling Johnny'. Behind the bronze globe of the Legion's Monument to the Dead is the museum. It is an Aladdin's cave of Legion treasures—uniforms, pistols, swords, paintings, decorations and a host of other objects—a rare feast for the historian and a delight for young boys. Adjudant-chef Szecsko is the museum's curator. Pale, almost ascetic in appearance, his long, thin fingers turn the pages of an ancient document or diary, in the hope of discovering some fresh aspect of Legion history.

Legio Patria Nostra (The Legion Is Our Fatherland) stands out in bold black letters on the wall of the Legion Museum. Meditate upon this motto, and on its chilling meaning. Frequently, Legionnaires have told me that they serve the Legion first, France second. Mystique is an overworked word, yet the only one to encompass everything about the Legion. Despite the reformation being carried out within the force, the old philosophies remain. Legion mystique is intoxicating, as all recruits soon learn. They are as willing today to embrace the words of General de Négrier as when they were first uttered over a century ago: 'You Legionnaires are soldiers in order to die—and I am sending you where you can die.'

General Coullon has something of an aristocratic quality about him, with a face that betrays a mischievous sense of humour. Quietly spoken, yet with no lack of authority in his manner, he commands the French Foreign Legion and the 31st Brigade from the tranquillity of his Aubagne office. You cannot help but feel his gentle charm when meeting him. Born in the wine country of the Loire, General Coullon has been a military man all his life, having graduated from Saint Cyr, France's foremost military college, in 1950. He has served in the Far East and North Africa, and recently commanded the French peace-keeping force in Beirut. He is a Legionnaire's general and, like all Legion officers, maintains a close relationship with his men. During the crisis in Beirut, his deep concern for his wounded Legionnaires was plain to see, as he visited them at the casualty clearing centre.

Stepping out into the bright spring sunlight, General Coullon walks briskly towards the line of Legionnaires standing smartly on the parade square. It is the ceremony of *libération*, which takes place each week for men taking their discharge. Within a few days, their képis packed at the bottom of their holdalls, together with new civilian outfits from the Legion's clothing shop, they will walk through the main gates into a world they left five or more years ago. Each Legionnaire comes to attention as the general approaches. He chats with them in turn before presenting the discharge certificates. Salutes are exchanged for the last time. Their days in the Legion are nearly over. There may be one or two who will return to the bosom of *la Légion*, having discovered that the outside world was not for them, and that, over the years, they have become inseparable from their adopted 'family'. Others will disappear into oblivion, find a new life, perhaps make a family of their own, but they will always carry in their hearts their days with the white képi.

It is hardly an extravagant observation to say that the Legion reflects the national character of France, regardless of certain segments of French society which refuse to admit that the Legion exists—that is, until it is needed. Oddly enough, it is the words of that British Consul's wife in a remote corner of Africa that best illustrate this paradox: 'It is a great relief to know that the Foreign Legion are just down the road.' As the Legion moves into the Euro-missile age, the 'family' must examine itself in a new light. Since its foundation in 1831, the Foreign Legion, as its name implies, has stood apart from France. A subtle but important change must now take place, for today's Legion must be more closely integrated within France and the French military network. I believe the Legion is on the verge of discovering this new balance, and for some time now the Legion 'fathers' have been searching for discreet ways of bringing about a fresh alignment of the family within French society, more fitting to the latter part of the twentieth century. At the same time, while many European armies are searching to accommodate a new form of military liberalism, by diluting the traditional forms of discipline, there is also a strong desire by the 'old school' within the Legion to adhere to the well-tried ways of relentless and unbending discipline of mind, as well as of body. Outside normal military circles, was not one of the world's finest 'armies' founded on these principles by Saint Ignatius Loyola—the Jesuits?

There will always be a need for men like those of the French Foreign Legion. The brotherhood of the white képi is a unique family. It will live on as long as there is adventure and courage in the hearts of men, for it would be difficult to imagine a world without them.

'When brothers agree, no fortress is so strong as their common life.' Antisthenes (5th/4th century BC).

The Legion's drums are carried lower than in other military bands.

Members of Old Comrades' Associations travel from all over the world to be at Aubagne for the Camerone celebrations.
Opposite: *The ceremony of libération. General Coullon presents the discharge certificate to a Legionnaire who is returning to civilian life.*

Camerone Remembered

Camerone Day, 30 April, marks the beginning of the Legion year and is one of the most important days in the calendar of every Legionnaire. It is also one of the few occasions in the year when the public can view the Legion and its traditions at close quarters. The Legion is becoming increasingly aware that the public gaze is more closely focused on it, now that it is based within metropolitan France. For the Legion, Camerone Day provides the opportunity to demonstrate that it is one of the finest fighting units in the world.

At Aubagne, several hundred

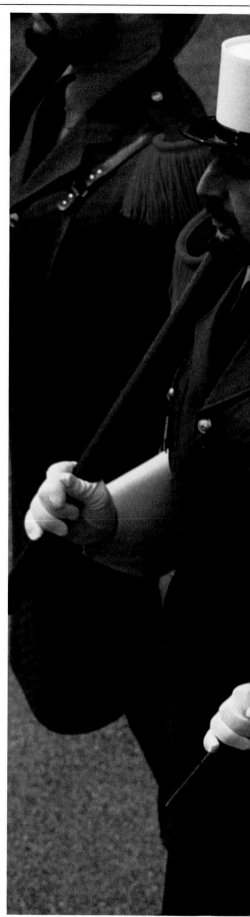

guests, from all parts of the community, are treated to a day of celebrations, following the traditional reading of the historic battle in distant Mexico. With a splash of colour, with marching, singing and music, the men of the Legion entertain their guests in the proudest military tradition. Bearded pioneers, wearing leather aprons and shouldering gleaming axes, contrast with the rows of Legionnaires standing to attention along the Sacred Way. Each year, the Camerone tradition is reenacted in every Legion regiment, wherever it may be.

Precision and dignity are the hallmarks of the annual Camerone festivities. Crowds listen in silent admiration to the haunting songs of the marching Legionnaires and to the music of their celebrated band (overleaf).

164

Major Roos, a highly decorated veteran of Indo-China and Algeria, is president of the sous-officiers' mess.
Opposite: *It is part of Legion tradition that pioneers are always bearded.*

The Colonel's Farewell

When Colonel Bertrand de La Presle was assigned to Paris at the end of his two-year command of the 1st REC, he was symbolically reduced to the rank of légionnaire before leaving the Quartier Labouche for the last time as the regiment's commanding officer. It was all part of Legion cavalry tradition. At the end of a hectic day of celebrations, the colonel's képi was replaced by a légionnaire's white one, and red epaulettes were placed on his shoulders. Drinking a final toast from a mess tin, he was bundled into a car, and driven off up the autoroute.

At least two generals, numerous colonels, the mayor and city fathers had all been invited to the festivities. An inspection parade and the presentation of medals follow a visit to the légionnaires' *foyer*. Families and friends tuck in to a cold buffet, followed by the singing of Legion songs. Finally, the colonel is toasted and presented with gifts by his officers. As the sun goes down, they stand erect and proudly sing *Le Boudin*.

Colonel B. de La Presle bids farewell to the 1st REC (preceding pages) *on leaving for a new appointment. After a day of festivities, and as the colonel makes his final departure, he is symbolically made a légionnaire, complete with white képi and red epaulettes.*

Corporal Johnny

'You must meet Paulin—he's one of your countrymen', said Colonel de La Presle.

He was short and stocky, with the rich accents of the north of England. 'The name's Paulin, but call me Corporal Johnny—everyone here knows who you mean', he said when we met. He wore a puckish smile, a cluster of campaign medals and the silver wings of a parachutist. He had served nearly twenty years with the Legion, and had seen plenty of action, especially in Algeria. Now he had only a few weeks remaining before his final departure. As we stood chatting about his many years as a Foreign Legionnaire, Corporal Johnny still looked every bit an Englishman. Perhaps it was the way he stood, with his square jaw jutting out and his hands behind his back. There was a hint of sadness in his manner as he spoke of his leaving. His Legion days had been good. He had made it to caporal-chef, which many old Legionnaires will tell you is an achievement. Johnny intended to return to England to see if he could settle down there. Perhaps he could, perhaps not. His Legion pension would enable him to spend a little time finding out.

A long-serving British Legionnaire, 'Corporal Johnny', who saw action in Algeria with the legendary 1st BEP. Overleaf: *Looking to the desert – a Legion veteran at Camerone.*

175

The Military Background.

REGIMENTAL HISTORIES

Historical summaries of the Foreign Legion's existing regiments.

1er Régiment Etranger/1st Foreign Regiment (1st RE) and Groupement de Légion Etrangère/Foreign Legion Group (GLE)

30 December 1840 Royal decree orders division of Foreign Legion into two Regiments, 1st and 2nd RE.

1 April 1841 Formation of 1st RE.

1843 Sidi-bel-Abbès settled by 1st RE.

1854/1855 1st and 2nd RE fight in Crimea as Foreign Brigade. 1st RE's commanding officer, Colonel Viénot, killed at Sebastopol.

1857 Pacification of Kabylia, Algeria.

1859 1st and 2nd RE fight in Italy (notably Magenta).

1862 1st RE amalgamated with 2nd RE to form single Foreign Regiment.

1863–1867 Mexican campaign.

30 April 1863 Battle of Camerone.

1870 Two battalions fight in France.

1875 Foreign Regiment renamed Foreign Legion.

1884/1885 Tonkin campaign (notably Tuyen Quang).

1885 Divided again into 1st and 2nd RE. Subsequent action in Dahomey, Sudan, Morocco, Madagascar and Algeria.

1906 Regimental colour of 1st RE awarded Legion of Honour.

1914 1st and 2nd RE form Régiments de Marche (Marching Regiments).

1915 Marching Regiments of 1st and 2nd RE amalgamated to form single Foreign Legion Marching Regiment (RMLE).

First World War Garibaldi Regiment (4th Marching Regiment of 1st RE) repatriated to Italy on that country's entry into the war. 1st and 2nd RE fight with Expeditionary Force at the Dardanelles.

1919–1939 1st RE continues fighting role, but also becomes training and administration unit of the Legion.

Second World War Croix de Guerre (1939–1945) awarded to colour of 1st RE.

1946 1st RE resumes role as home base for the whole Foreign Legion, as training school and as reception centre for home-coming troops.

1946–1956 1st RE provides large training base for forces for Indo-China.

1954 1st RE resumes operational role in Algeria, at Sidi-bel-Abbès, Saïda, Mascara, and Bedeau.

1962 1st RE leaves Sidi-bel-Abbès at end of Algerian war. Bodies of General Rollet, Prince Aage of Denmark and Légionnaire Zimmermann reburied at Puyloubier, Provence.

26 October 1962 New base established at Aubagne and Training Corps stationed in Corsica.

1 September 1972 Regiment divided once more. 1st RE remains in mainland France, 2nd RE in Corsica, with newly created Operational Group (GOLE). GLE formed; responsible for administration and training of all non-commissioned ranks. Authority of its commanding officer applies to all units of the Legion.

1976 Training companies leave Corsica for Castelnaudary. Temporarily attached to 1st RE.

1 September 1977 Régiment d'Instruction de Légion Etrangère/Foreign Legion Training Regiment (RILE) formed.

REGIMENTAL COLOUR OF THE 1ST RE
Battle honours on the flag:

Sebastopol	1855
Kabylia	1857
Magenta	1859
Camerone	1863
Far East	1884–1885
Dahomey–Morocco	1892–1907–1925
Madagascar	1895–1905
Eastern Front	1915–1917

Pinned to the cravat: Cross of the Legion of Honour
Croix de Guerre (1939–1945)
Commemorative Medal of the City of Milan.

THE 1ST RE IN 1983
Directly under the orders of the general commanding the GLE, the 1st RE has an extremely versatile role, with responsibilities throughout the world. Its duties include:
Administrative support for communal staff

The graves of General Rollet and Prince Aage of Denmark in the cemetery at Sidi-bel-Abbès. On 29 September 1962, their bodies were exhumed, with that of Légionnaire Zimmermann, and taken to France for reburial in the Legion cemetery at Puyloubier.

throughout the Foreign Legion
Administration of unattached non-commissioned personnel
Passenger transport
Earthworks for Canjuers Camp and the 5th Military Region
Defence of the Albion plateau.

The main body of the 1st RE is at Aubagne. There are also a company at Canjuers (engaged in roadworks), a Transport Company in Paris, and many small detachments throughout France, serving as information offices of the Legion.

2e Régiment Etranger d'Infanterie/2nd Foreign Infantry Regiment (2nd REI)

21 April 1841 Formation of 2nd RE. Fights in Algeria (Algiers and Oran).
June 1854 Forms Foreign Brigade with units of 1st RE in Crimea. Gains honours at Alma and Sebastopol. Returns to Algeria.
1859 Goes to Italy. Commanding officer, Colonel de Chabrière, killed at Magenta.
14 August 1859 Takes part in victory parade in Paris.
1862 Amalgamates with 1st RE to become single Foreign Regiment. Fights gloriously in Mexico (see 1st RE).
1885 2nd RE re-formed in Algeria.
1886 Establishes base at Saïda; subsequently sees action in South Oran, Tonkin, Dahomey, Sudan, Madagascar and Morocco.
First World War Contributes battalion to Expeditionary Force for Eastern Front and Marching Regiment for French Front.
1920 Leaves Saïda for Meknes, Morocco. Subsequently in action in Taza region, the Rif and Atlas mountains.
1943 2nd RE temporarily disbanded to supply men to units fighting in France.
1945 Regiment re-formed as 2nd REI; departs immediately for Far East.
1945–1955 Fights in Cochin China, Annam and Tonkin. First battalion almost annihilated at Dien Bien Phu. Losses rewarded by two mentions in dispatches and lanyard of the Croix de Guerre (Overseas Operations).
1955–1962 Regiment returns to Algeria, then moves to Morocco and the Sahara—its sphere of operations for next eleven years.
October 1962 Leaves Aïn Sefra sector for Colomb Béchar, attached to Saharan Military Sites Command. Takes up quarters at Mers-el-Kebir after end of nuclear experiments.
31 January 1968 Temporary disbandment of 2nd REI when Mers-el-Kebir (last French base in North Africa) abandoned.
1 September 1972 2nd RE re-formed from units of 1st RE based in Corsica.
February 1976 Sent to Djibouti at time of Loyada incident.
1978–1979 In action in Chad.
1 June 1980 Readopts name of 2nd REI.
July 1982 With Multi-National Peacekeeping Force in Beirut.

REGIMENTAL COLOUR OF THE 2ND REI
Battle honours on the flag:

Sebastopol	1855
Kabylia	1857
Magenta	1859
Camerone	1863
Far East	1884–1885
Dahomey	1892
Madagascar	1898–1905
Morocco	1907–1913, 1921–1934
Indo-China	1946–1954

The colour bears the lanyard of the Croix de Guerre (Overseas Operations).
Pinned to the cravat: Croix de Guerre (Overseas Operations)
Commemorative Medal of the City of Milan.

THE 2ND REI IN 1983
With 1500 men, the regiment has two separate functions:
Training of officers, NCOs and men, as well as of specialist forces—all the responsibility of the Foreign Legion Training Group (GILE).
Overseas action—the responsibility of the Foreign Legion Operational Group (GOLE).
The regiment recently left the garrison towns of Corte and Bonifacio in Corsica (November 1983) to settle in Nîmes. This transfer was part of the general reorganization of the army.

3e Régiment Etranger d'Infanterie/3rd Foreign Infantry Regiment (3rd REI)

11 November 1915 Foreign Legion Marching Regiment (RMLE) formed from remnants of Marching Regiments of 1st and 2nd RE, which had suffered heavy casualties in early battles of World War I.
1915–1918 Gains glory in much of the fiercest fighting of the war.
14 September 1918 Under command of Lt-col. Rollet, succeeds in piercing Hindenburg Line. RMLE awarded Cross of the Legion of Honour, Military Medal and double lanyard, having suffered very heavy casualties.
1 January 1921 RMLE becomes 3rd REI.
1920–1934 3rd REI active in pacification of Morocco, sustaining heavy losses, and subsequently in building and development projects throughout the country.
1928 Sapper-Pioneer Company pierces famous Foum-Zabel tunnel in Morocco.
1942–1943 3rd REI fights Afrika Korps in Tunisia, alongside Americans.

Legionnaire in full-dress uniform, 1831–35.

Sergent porte-fanion (colour sergeant) of a Legion company of the 1st Marching Regiment of Africa, Eastern Front, 1917. Opposite: *Legionnaire in Spain, 1835–39.*

24 June 1943 3rd REI disbanded.
1 July 1943 RMLE re-formed from elements of 3rd REI and 1st REIM. Fights with 5th Armoured Division in liberation of France and in Alsace campaign; crosses the Rhine and thrusts as far as Austria. Awarded three mentions in dispatches.
2 July 1945 RMLE resumes name of 3rd REI.
25 April 1946 3rd REI arrives in Indo-China. Involved in heavy fighting at Phu

Tong Hoa, Dong Khe, Cao Bang and Dien Bien Phu. Suffers severe losses in Indo-China campaign and is awarded lanyard of Military Medal (Overseas Operations).

1 June 1949 Parachute Company of 3rd REI (formed 1 April 1948) transferred to 1st BEP.

1954 Leaves Indo-China for Algeria.

1954–1962 3rd REI involved in large-scale operations throughout Algeria, at first in Aurès mountains, then North Constantine and the Tunisian border.

1962–1973 Regiment stationed in Madagascar. Specializes in amphibious operations and develops training for tropical conditions.

1973 3rd REI sails for French Guiana. Involved there in vast roadworks and training for jungle fighting.

REGIMENTAL COLOUR OF THE 3RD REI
Battle honours on the flag:

Camerone	1863
Artois	1915
Champagne	1915
Somme	1916
Heights of Verdun	1917
Picardy-Soissons	1918
Vauxaillon	1918
Morocco	1921–1934
Djebel Mansour	1943
Alsace	1944–1945
Stuttgart	1945
Indo-China	1946–1954

Decorated with: Lanyard in colour of ribbon of the Legion of Honour with one white-banded olive in colours of ribbon of the Croix de Guerre (1914–1918) and of the Legion of Honour, and one olive in colours of ribbon of the Croix de Guerre (1939–1945)
Lanyard in colours of ribbon of the Military Medal with olive in colours of ribbon of the Croix de Guerre (Overseas Operations)
Lanyard in colours of ribbon of the Croix de Guerre (1914–1918).
Pinned to the cravat: Cross of the Legion of Honour
Military Medal
Croix de Guerre (1914–1918) with nine mentions in dispatches
Croix de Guerre (1939–1945) with three mentions in dispatches
Croix de Guerre (Overseas Operations) with four mentions in dispatches
Moroccan Military Merit (Mérite Militaire Chérifien)
Order of the Tower and Sword of Portugal
Catalan Volunteers' Medal
Distinguished Unit Badge.

THE 3RD REI IN 1983
Since its arrival in French Guiana in 1973, some 3200 Legionnaires have completed two-year postings there with the 3rd REI. Their work is mostly deep in the jungle, where they have opened up some 125

miles of tracks and surfaced roads—in particular, the Route de l'Est (Eastern Highway), which will link Cayenne to Saint-Georges. They are also responsible for the security of the Ariane rocket site at Kourou.

The 3rd REI consists of four companies, three of them based at the European Space Station at Kourou and the fourth at Camp Szuts, Régina.

4e Régiment Etranger/4th Foreign Regiment (4th RE)

15 November 1920 4th Foreign Infantry Regiment (4th REI) formed in Morocco.

1920–1926 Some battalions sent to Lebanon and Syria to fight the Druzes. Three remain for pacification of Morocco.

1935 Pacification of Morocco completed after twenty years of fighting. Regiment begins work on infrastructure and development of South Morocco.

1 September 1939 4th REI supplies most of the men for 11th and 12th RE, stationed in France, and then for 13th Foreign Legion Half-Brigade (13th DBLE).

14 November 1940 4th REI disbanded.

15 August 1941 4th Foreign Legion Half-Brigade (4th DBLE) formed. Adopts regimental colour of 4th REI (21 August). Settles firstly in Senegal and later takes important part in Tunisian campaign.

16 April 1943 4th DBLE takes name of 1st Foreign Marching Infantry Regiment (1st REIM) and fights at Djebel Mansour. At end of Tunisian campaign, receives battle honour of Djebel Zaghouan and Croix de Guerre (1939–1945) with palm.

3 June 1943 1st REIM disbanded.

16 May 1946 4th Foreign Legion Half-Brigade of Morocco formed.

1947–1951 One battalion sent to Madagascar to restore order.

16 October 1948 Regiment resumes name of 4th REI.

1952–1956 4th REI performs peace-keeping role in Morocco.

1957 Finally leaves Morocco for Algeria.

1956–1964 4th REI active on Algerian-Tunisian border. After cease-fire, travels throughout Sahara.

30 April 1964 4th REI disbanded.

1 June 1980 4th RE re-formed at Castelnaudary as training regiment, taking over from Foreign Legion Training Regiment (RILE), which had been formed in 1977.

REGIMENTAL COLOUR OF THE 4TH RE
Battle honours on the flag:

Camerone	1863
Morocco	1914–1918, 1921–1934
Djebel Zaghouan	1943

Pinned to the cravat: Croix de Guerre (1939–1945) with one mention in dispatches.

THE 4TH RE IN 1983
The 4th RE has its headquarters, Command and Services Company, two Recruit Companies and NCO Training Company based in the Quartier Lapasset at Castelnaudary. It is responsible for the basic training of new recruits and further training of NCOs.

Outside the town, the regiment has a firing range and assault course.

Each company also has its own farm and training grounds.

In 1984, a start is being made on new quarters, 'Les Cheminières'. These will provide barrack accommodation, as well as firing ranges and sports grounds outside Castelnaudary.

5e Régiment Mixte du Pacifique/ 5th Mixed Pacific Regiment (5th RMP)

1 September 1930 5th Foreign Infantry Regiment (5th REI) formed from four Foreign Legion battalions operating in Indo-China.

1940 5th REI in action against Japanese.

1941 In action against Thais.

9 March 1945 Japanese attack French forces and inflict heavy losses. Legionnaires fight at Ha Giang, Lang Son and Hanoi, but are overwhelmed by numbers. Succeed in breaking out at Cottich and join 'Tong Group', formed round 1st and 2nd Battalions of 5th REI. After dramatic 1250-mile retreat, survivors regroup at Tsao Pa in Yunnan.

1 July 1945 Regiment disbanded, having lost two-thirds of its men. Becomes Marching Battalion of 5th REI.

1946 Caught between Chinese troops and the new Viet Minh enemy, battalion manages to reach Laos and the Mekong Valley.

November 1946 Battalion repatriated to Sidi-bel-Abbès and disbanded (20 January 1947).

July 1949 5th REI re-formed. Fights in all campaigns in Tonkin, Central Annam and Laos.

1954 Towards end of year, regiment assembles in Annam and then in Cap St. Jacques region, having abandoned bases the Legion had occupied in all parts of Indo-China.

1956 2nd Battalion of 5th REI is last Legion unit to leave Far East. Regiment settles in Algeria, where responsibilities include Marnia-Nédroma sector, then Turenne and Hafir regions. Engaged in fighting rebels and in protecting agriculture and sensitive areas.

July 1957 5th REI reduced to two battalions: 1st and 3rd.

1958 Organized into 'intervention force' to go in hot pursuit of enemy.

1959 Regiment at Ouarsenis (in Greater Kabylia), then protecting cork harvest in Collo peninsula.

1960 Guarding Algerian-Tunisian border.

1961 Active on Algerian-Moroccan border, then in Géryville region.

1962 After cease-fire, 5th REI stationed in Colomb Béchar and Aïn Sefra region, in south of Algeria.

June 1963 First Legion detachments sent to Tahiti.

September 1963 First detachment installed on Mururoa.

1 October 1963 Following decision of the Ministry of Defence in August 1963, 5th RMP is formed as engineering unit to work on Pacific Test Centre. New regiment inherits traditions of 5th REI, whose colour it receives on 9 December 1963, after disbandment of 5th REI on 30 November.

1964 5th RMP sets up sites on Tahiti, Mururoa, Hao and Rapa.

1965–1968 Construction sites established on atolls throughout French Polynesia. Regiment responsible for maintenance of vehicles and machinery of Pacific Test Centre, and for operation of power stations and production of fresh water. Companies reorganized in July 1968 to meet the new demands.

24 August 1968 First French nuclear bomb successfully tested.

1969–1975 More and more substantial works on other atolls scattered over thousands of square miles of the Pacific lead to another reorganization of the regiment.

1976 5th RMP concentrates all its elements on Mururoa. Electro-Mechanical Company becomes Water Power Company, and a Support Company is formed and based on Hao.

1977 Support Company disbanded and its resources transferred to other companies on Mururoa. Only very small detachments remain on outlying atolls. A small transport unit and a section of the Water Power Company remain on Tahiti.

REGIMENTAL COLOUR OF THE 5TH RMP
Battle honours on the flag:

Camerone	1863
Son Tay	1883
Bac Ninh	1884
Tuyen Quang	1885
Lang Son	1885
Indo-China	1945–1946, 1949–1954

Decorated with: Lanyard of the Croix de Guerre (Overseas Operations).
Pinned to the cravat: Croix de Guerre (1939–1945) with one mention in dispatches
Croix de Guerre (Overseas Operations) with two mentions in dispatches.

THE 5TH RMP IN 1983
Today, it is the 5th RMP that maintains the French presence in the Pacific, although its final reorganization marked the end of the time when the regiment was represented in every corner of French Polynesia.

During its nineteen years in the region, the regiment's achievements have been substantial, considering the difficulties involved in operating in this vast area of the Pacific, where the hard reality of life is far removed from the romantic notions of popular fiction. Long, uncomfortable sea journeys, heat, separation and isolation are among the everyday hardships that the Legionnaires must live with.

13e Demi-Brigade de Légion Etrangère/13th Foreign Legion Half-Brigade (13th DBLE)

20 February 1940 13th DBLE formed at Sidi-bel-Abbès, Algeria.

13 May 1940 Lands on northern coast of Norway, captures Bjervik and Narvik, and pushes enemy back to Swedish frontier. Hurriedly recalled when situation in France deteriorates.

14 June 1940 Arrives in Brest, then taken to England to join de Gaulle's forces. After reorganization and retraining, 13th DBLE is sent to Cameroon and Gabon as part of 1st Free French Division.

27 March 1941 Takes part in capture of Keren, Eritrea.

7 April 1941 Takes part in capture of Massawa, taking 14,000 prisoners.

May 1941 Arrives in Ismailia, Egypt, for operations in Palestine and Syria.

December 1941 13th DBLE reorganized, reinforced and sent back to Egypt. Then, in 1942, goes to relieve a British unit in Libya.

27 May 1942 First battle of Bir Hakeim.

10 June 1942 Garrison breaks out of Bir Hakeim through beseiging forces, suffering heavy losses.

October 1942 After regrouping in Cairo, 13th DBLE occupies position south of El Alamein and takes part in attack on El Himeimat peak. Lt-col. Prince Amilakvari killed in the action. After further reorganization in Tobruk region, unit is sent to Tunisia.

13 May 1943 Takes Takrouna, then settles on Gulf of Hammamet for reinforcements and reequipment.

April 1944 13th DBLE lands at Naples, takes part in Garigliano offensive, passes through Rome and captures Radicofani.

16 August 1944 Advance sections land on French soil at Cavalaire. 13th DBLE takes part in capture of Toulon, then marches on Aix and Avignon before liberating Autun and reaching the Belfort region. After hard fighting in Vosges campaign, 13th DBLE is sent to Atlantic front and then to Alsace to halt the push towards Strasbourg.

23 January 1945 Takes part in liberation of Colmar, then presses on to the Rhine (early February).

March 1945 Moved to southeast France, seizes Authion mountains and opens Colle di Tende pass to Italy.

May 1945 In Italy when war ends.

August 1945 Embarks for North Africa.

December 1945 Posted to Far East.

March 1946 Once again on war footing, 13th DBLE arrives in Indo-China.

1946–1951 Engaged in operations in Cochin China, Cambodia and Central Annam.

1951–1952 Heroic actions in Tonkin include Hoa Binh, Xom Pheo and defence of Na San.

1953 Command Company, 1st and 3rd Battalions sent to Dien Bien Phu, where they fight to near extinction. 2nd Battalion gains total success in fierce fighting in Mekong Delta.

May 1954 After fall of Dien Bien Phu, 13th DBLE re-formed as rearguard of Land Forces of North Vietnam.

June 1955 Returns to North Africa after brief stay in South Vietnam.

1955–1962 Engaged in military action and pacification in Algeria—in Constantine Province, the Nementcha and the Aurès. Becomes intervention regiment in 1958, active throughout Algeria.

September–October 1962 13th DBLE regroups in French Somaliland, which becomes French Territory of the Afars and Issas in 1967.

June 1977 When Territory becomes independent as Republic of Djibouti, 13th DBLE remains as part of French forces stationed there by treaty with the Republic.

26th August 1978 1st Company disbanded.

15th October 1979 4th Company disbanded. Despite disbandment of these fighting units, overall fire-power has been increased by creation of a Heavy Mortar Section and a Milan (anti-tank missile) Section.

REGIMENTAL COLOUR OF THE 13TH DBLE
Battle honours on the flag:

Camerone	1863
Bjervik-Narvik	1940
Keren-Massawa	1941
Bir Hakeim	1942
El Alamein	1942
Rome	1944
Colmar	1945
Authion	1945
Indo-China	1946–1954

Decorated with: Lanyard of the Military Medal with olive in colours of the Military Medal and of the Croix de Guerre (1939–1945)
Lanyard of the Military Medal with olive in colours of the Croix de Guerre (Overseas Operations).
Pinned to the cravat: Cross of Companion of the Liberation
Rosette of the Resistance

Croix de Guerre (1939–1945) with four
mentions in dispatches
Croix de Guerre (Overseas Operations)
with four mentions in dispatches
Croix de Guerre (Norway) with sword.

THE 13TH DBLE IN 1983

The 13th DBLE is an inter-arm formation
comprising four basic units, reinforced by
a rotating company of the 2nd REP, for
which it provides support. The four units,
all armed with the most up-to-date
weapons and equipment, are:

Command and Services Company

Works Company (2nd Company)

Combat Company (3rd Company)

Reconnaissance Squadron.

As part of the French Forces Stationed in

The Foreign Legion's cap badges. Top: *infantry
(worn by 1st RE, 2nd REI, 3rd REI, 4th RE,
5th RMP, 13th DBLE and DLEM).* Bottom
left: *cavalry (worn by 1st REC).* Bottom right:
parachutists (worn by 2nd REP).

*Bugler of the 1st RE, 1931. Opposite:
Drummer of the 2nd RE, 1931. Overleaf:
Camerone Day parade at Sidi-bel-Abbès,
30 April, 1960.*

Insignia of the Foreign Legion's existing regiments. Top row, left to right: *1st RE, 13th DBLE, 4th
RE.* Second row, left to right: *5th RMP, GLE, 3rd REI.* Third row, left to right: *DLEM, 1st REC,
2nd REP.* Bottom: *2nd REI.*

Djibouti, its duties are to guarantee the
defence, territorial integrity and
independence of the Republic of Djibouti.
The Legionnaires maintain their
operational readiness by 'bush tours' and
'nomadization', regimental exercises, and
amphibious training.

1er Régiment Etranger de Cavalerie/1st Foreign Cavalry Regiment (1st REC)

1921 1st REC formed in Tunisia from
elements of 2nd REI, together with some
French officers and NCOs from cavalry
regiments of the French army and large
numbers of Russian political exiles (mostly
from Wrangel's White Army).

1925 In action simultaneously in Syria
and Morocco. Landriau squadron awarded
Overseas Operations lanyard (fourragère
des TOE—Théâtres d'Opérations
Extérieurs).

1927–1934 Engaged in pacification of
Morocco and Algeria, firstly in a fighting
capacity, then ensuring security of
Saharan routes being developed by
Lyautey.

18 May 1940 Regiment in action on the
Somme, under name of Divisional
Reconnaissance Group 97, until armistice.
Mentioned in dispatches for its heroism.

1943 Survivors of battles of 1940 return
to Africa and fight against Germans in
Tunisia.

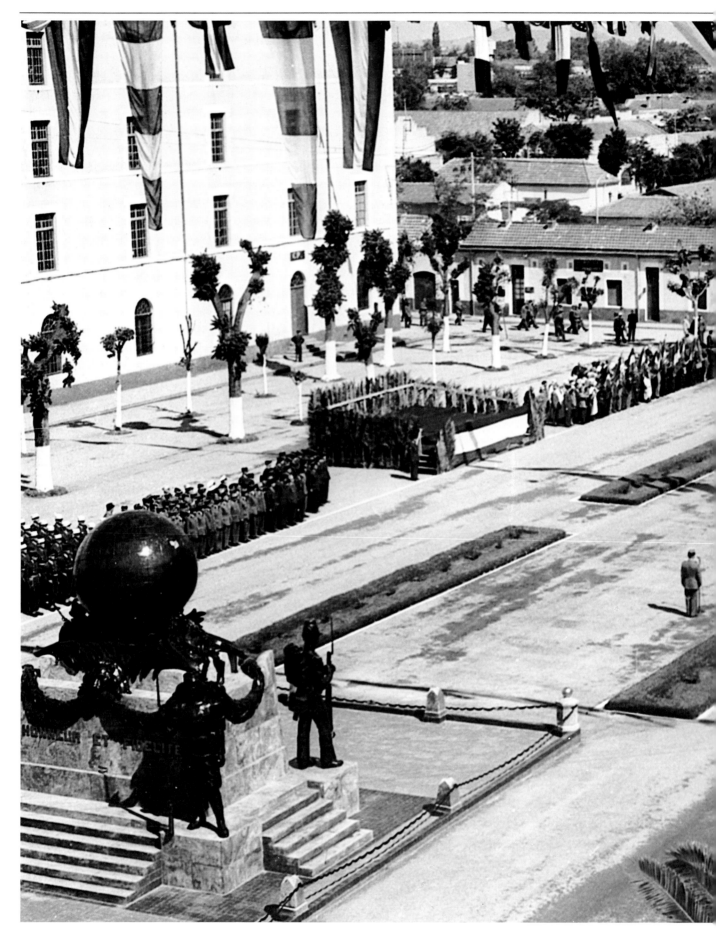

1944 1st REC lands on coast of Provence and fights for liberation of France. Enters Germany at head of French armoured units.

1945 At end of war, regimental standard awarded three palms and lanyard of the Croix de Guerre (1939–1945).

1945–1954 1st REC, with two amphibious units, engaged in Indo-China campaign, from Cochin China to Tonkin. Receives further decorations for heroism.

1954–1962 Regiment returns to North Africa and takes part in pacification of Algeria.

1962–1967 Remains in Algeria after cease-fire and Evian peace agreement, based at Mers-el-Kebir.

17 October 1967 For first time in its history, 1st REC settles in France, at Orange (Quartier Labouche).

REGIMENTAL STANDARD OF THE 1ST REC
Battle honours on the flag:

Camerone	1863
Levant	1925–1926
Morocco	1925–1927, 1930–1934
Ousseltia	1943
Colmar	1945
Stuttgart	1945
Indo-China	1947–1954

Pinned to the cravat: Croix de Guerre (1939–1945) with three palms (Tunisia 1943, Alsace 1944, Karlsruhe-Stuttgart 1945)
Croix de Guerre (Overseas Operations) with three palms
Lanyard of the Croix de Guerre (1939–1945)
Lanyard of the Croix de Guerre (Overseas Operations).

THE 1ST REC IN 1983
The 1st REC is an armoured regiment of the 14th Infantry Division, and is involved in all the Division's missions as part of the Territorial Operational Defence. It also provides reinforcements for the 1st Army, when necessary. As part of the Overseas Action Force, the 4th Squadron was sent to Djibouti in 1976 with the 2nd RE's Operational Group (GOLE). The regiment rotates regularly between postings in Africa and Mayotte.

During 1984, the 1st REC will cease to be part of the 14th Infantry Division. It will then relieve the 5th Light Armoured Division, an important unit of the army's Rapid Action Force.

2e Régiment Etranger de Parachutistes/2nd Foreign Parachute Regiment (2nd REP)

1948 First Foreign Legion parachute units formed.

1 April 1948 3rd REI raises Parachute Company in Indo-China from men of 2nd and 3rd REI and 13th DBLE. Goes into action immediately.

1 July 1948 1st Foreign Parachute Battalion (1st BEP) formed at Khamisis, Algeria.

12 November 1948 1st BEP arrives at Haiphong, Indo-China.

2 October 1948 First companies of 2nd BEP formed at Sidi-bel-Abbès and in Morocco. New battalion regroups at Sétif, Algeria, and receives its banner (fanion).

8 February 1949 2nd BEP posted to Indo-China.

June 1949 1st BEP absorbs Parachute Company of 3rd REI.

1949 3rd BEP formed in Algeria to train men for 1st and 2nd BEP.

1949–1954 1st and 2nd BEP involved in all heaviest fighting in Indo-China (from RC 4 to Dien Bien Phu), reinforced by Foreign Air Supply Company in 1951 and Foreign Heavy Mortar Parachute Company in 1953.

1 December 1955 2nd BEP returns to Algeria, having received Croix de Guerre (Overseas Operations) with six mentions in dispatches. Battalion's Legionnaires granted distinction (unique in the Expeditionary Force) of wearing lanyard of the Legion of Honour.

5 June 1956 As 2nd REP, receives its regimental colour, after absorbing 3rd BEP and becoming a regiment.

1956–1962 Heavily involved in Algerian campaign as part of 25th Parachute Division.

1962 Lengthy and wide-ranging intervention in Chad.

1970 2nd REP regroups at Calvi, Corsica. Resumes training, while maintaining rotating company in Djibouti.

February 1976 During one of its tours of duty in Djibouti, 2nd Company takes part in freeing of children held hostage in Loyada, Somalia.

1978 Regiment again in action in Chad, where one of its training units is involved in fighting at Djeeda and Ati.

18 May 1978 2nd REP receives orders to intervene in Kolwezi, Zaïre.

19 May 1978 Carries out parachute raid on Kolwezi and completes successful rescue mission. 2nd REP earns worldwide praise and seventh mention in dispatches.

REGIMENTAL COLOUR OF THE 2ND REP
Battle honours on the flag:

Camerone	1863
Indo-China	1949–1954

Decorated with: Lanyard of the Legion of Honour, its olive in the colours of the ribbon of the Croix de Guerre (Overseas Operations).
Pinned to the cravat: Croix de Guerre (Overseas Operations) with seven mentions in dispatches.

THE 2ND REP IN 1983
The 2nd REP is at present the only parachute unit of the Foreign Legion, providing a unique combination of Legion discipline and paratroop flexibility.

The regiment remains on full-time alert for instant action in all overseas theatres of operations.

The 1300 officers and men of the 2nd REP are divided into six companies:
One Command and Services Company
One Scouting and Support Company
Four Combat Companies.

Détachement de Légion Etrangère de Mayotte/Foreign Legion Detachment of Mayotte (DLEM)

November 1967 First Legionnaires arrive on Comoro Islands. Detachment comprises a company of the 3rd REI from Madagascar, which sets up bases on the rock of Dzaoudzi (on the small island of Pamandze off Mayotte) and also at Moroni (the islands' capital on Great Comoro).

1 August 1973 When 3rd REI leaves for French Guiana, unit takes name of Foreign Legion Detachment of the Comoros (DLEC).

1 April 1976 After independence of the Comoros (when Mayotte chose to become an overseas department of France), detachment changes name to Foreign Legion Detachment of Mayotte (DLEM) and remains at Dzaoudzi. Another site subsequently acquired at Kwale for new barracks.

THE DLEM IN 1983
With a population of some fifty thousand, Mayotte occupies a strategic position at the opening of the Mozambique Channel into the Indian Ocean. The responsibility of the DLEM is to affirm French sovereignty on the island, to provide security, and to support the civil and military authorities in maintaining the French way of life.

The commanding officer of the DLEM is commander of all military forces on Mayotte, including naval and air support. The military authority also guarantees fuel supplies by means of a permanent oil depot on the island.

In addition to construction, supply and security duties, the DLEM is kept in constant operational readiness by regular exercises, target practice and amphibious training.

LEGION ETRANGERE
(March 1831–December 1840)

FIRST FORMATION
(March 1831–June 1835)

OLD LEGION

Stoffel, Colonel, 4 May 1831.
Combe, Colonel, 1 April 1832. Killed in the assault on Constantine.
De Mollenbeck (pro tem.), 18 October 1832 (Lieutenant-colonel: 48th of Line).
Bernelle (pro tem.), 9 November 1832 (Lieutenant-colonel: 10th of Line).
Bernelle, 9 April 1833.

(IN THE SERVICE OF SPAIN)

Bernelle, Maréchal de camp, Spanish title, 30 June 1835.
Lebeau, Maréchal de camp, Spanish title, 30 August 1836.
Conrad, Maréchal de camp, Spanish title, 10 November 1836. Killed at Barbastro, 2 June 1837.

SECOND FORMATION
(December 1835–December 1840)

NEW LEGION

Bedeau, Chef de bataillon, 3 February 1836. Sole battalion.
De Hulsen, Colonel, 2 August 1837 (regiment re-formed 18 July 1837). Died of fever at Fondouk, December 1840.

1er AND 2e REGIMENTS DE LA LEGION ETRANGERE
(January 1841–April 1856)

From January 1855, they become 1er and 2e Régiments de la 1re Légion Etrangère

1er REGIMENT

De Mollenbeck, 1 April 1841.
Despinoy, 8 April 1842.
Mouret, 10 February 1843.
Mellinet, 15 March 1846.
Lesueur de Givry (exchange), 4 December 1850.
Bazaine, 4 February 1851.
Viénot, 5 September 1854 (killed at Sebastopol, 2 May 1855).
Lévy (exchange), 26 May 1855.
Martenot de Cordoue, 23 September 1855.

2e REGIMENT

De Senilhe, 21 April 1841.
De MacMahon, Lieutenant-colonel, 1843–1844.
De Senilhe, 1844–1847.
D'Autemarre, June 1845.
Certain-Canrobert, 18 January 1848.
De Noue, 15 June 1848.
Carbuccia, 31 August 1848. Died of cholera in 1854 as General

Commanding 1re Légion Etrangère.
Coeur, 26 February 1851.
De Caprez, 24 December 1851–30 May 1855.
De Granet Lacroix de Chabrière, 30 May 1855.

2e LEGION ETRANGERE
1er AND 2e REGIMENTS ETRANGERS
(Swiss Legion 1855–1856)

Formed in France.
Commanded by the honorary Swiss General Ochsenbein, a personal friend of Napoleon III.

Meyer, Colonel, 1er Régiment, 3 February 1855.
De Granet Lacroix de Chabrière, 2e Régiment, 3 February 1855.
De Caprez, 2e Régiment, in exchange with the former, 30 May 1855.
Lion, Chef de bataillon, battalion of Tirailleurs, 28 February 1855.

1er AND 2e REGIMENTS ETRANGERS (1856–1862)

1er REGIMENT

Meyer, 5 June 1856.
De Saint-André, 2 August 1858.

Granchetti (retired), 28 August 1858.
Brayer, 7 November 1858.
Martinez, 5 December 1859.

2e REGIMENT

De Granet Lacroix de Chabrière, 30 May 1855. Killed 29 June 1859 at Magenta.
Martinez (pro tem.), 30 May 1859.
Signorino (exchange), 20 August 1859.
Butet, 19 October 1859.

REGIMENT ETRANGER
(1862–1875)

Butet, from 2e Régiment. Retained.
Jeanningros, 15 March 1862.
Lavoignet (exchange), 13 August 1865.
D'Ornano, 18 August 1865.
Jeanningros, Général, 11 June 1866.
De Courcy (exchange), 17 January 1866.
Guilhem (killed in the siege of Paris, 30 September 1870).
Deplanque, 25 August 1867.
De Curten, 4 October 1870.
Thierry (exchange), 25 November 1870.
Chaulan (exchange), 1 January 1871.
De Mallaret, 17 January 1871–1881.

LEGION ETRANGERE
(1875–1884)

De Mallaret, from 2e Régiment Etranger,

Colonel Combe, commander of the Foreign Legion in 1832. He was killed in the assault on Constantine, 13 October 1837.

17 January 1871.
De Négrier, 7 July 1881.
Grisot, 11 September 1883.

1er AND 2e REGIMENTS ETRANGERS (From 1885)

1er REGIMENT

Grisot, 1 January 1885 (from the Légion Etrangère).
Watringue, 14 October 1886.
Barberet, 12 February 1890.
Zeni, 12 March 1891.
De Villebois-Mareuil, 14 April 1895. General of the Transvaal. Killed in action.
Bertrand, 6 April 1896.
Dautelle, 29 August 1900.
Boutegourd, 23 September 1904.
Girardot, 23 March 1907.
Bavouzet, 24 December 1910.
Boyer, 23 September 1913.
Cosman, Lieutenant-colonel, 22 April 1914.
Met, Lieutenant-colonel, 21 March 1915.
Heliot, Lieutenant-colonel, 3 September 1916.
Forey, Lieutenant-colonel, 21 September 1918.
Riet, Chef de bataillon, September 1919.
Boulet-Desbarreau, Colonel, 23 April 1920.
Rollet, Colonel, 9 September 1925.
Nicolas, Colonel, 26 March 1931.
Maire, 17 April 1934.
Debas, 22 November 1934.
Azan, 16 February 1935.
Robert, 23 April 1939.
Flan, 21 February 1940.
Girard, 6 March 1940.
Bouty, 5 October 1940.
Lambert, 15 August 1941.
Barre, 1 December 1941.
Vias, 1 April 1942.
Gaultier, 1 January 1946.
Pénicaut, 1 September 1950.
Thomas, 3 April 1953.
Raberin, 1 July 1955.
Lemeunier, Colonel (pro tem.), 11 November 1956.
Thomas, Colonel, 27 November 1956.
Brothier, Colonel, 16 May 1959.
Vaillant, Colonel, 26 August 1961.
Vadot, Colonel, 28 June 1963.
Chenel, Colonel, 6 August 1966.
Fuhr, Colonel, 5 September 1968.
Letestu, Colonel, 20 August 1970.
Plantevin, Lieutenant-colonel, 1 September 1972.
Riou, Lieutenant-colonel, 30 August 1974.
Delsuc, Lieutenant-colonel, 1 September 1976.
Thibout, Lieutenant-colonel, 1 October 1976.
Ameline, Colonel, 26 September 1978.
Talbourdet, Lieutenant-colonel, 13 September 1980.
Bénézit, Lieutenant-colonel, 1 September 1982.

General de Gaulle visiting the Quartier Viénot at Sidi-bel-Abbès, 2 July 1958.

2e REGIMENT

Hugot, 1 January 1885.
Letellier, 21 May 1886.
Vincent, 3 June 1888.
Gillet, 28 December 1889.
Oudri, 22 March 1893.
Gosse-Dubois, 8 May 1895.
Kerdrain, 26 June 1896.
Béranger, 18 November 1896.
Bruneau, 19 June 1900.
Deshortes, 17 November 1902.
Schlumberger, 18 November 1906.
Branlière, 22 January 1908.
Alix, 19 April 1908.
Brulard, 25 December 1908.
Passard, 9 July 1911. Left in 1914 with the Régiment Mobilisé, 2e Régiment de Marche du 2e Etranger.
Bourgeois, 17 September 1914.
Plaude, 12 March 1915, Saïda headquarters.
Arque, Chef de bataillon, 19 October 1915, Saïda headquarters.
Deville, Chef de bataillon, 21 October 1915, Saïda headquarters.
Donnève, Chef de bataillon, 15 July 1916, Saïda headquarters.
Chartier, Lieutenant-colonel, 3 April 1917, Saïda headquarters.
Adrien, Chef de bataillon, 2 July 1917, Saïda headquarters.

Hottenger, Chef de bataillon, 30 August 1918, Saïda headquarters.
Martin, Colonel, 19 May 1920. Regiment re-formed at Saïda, then in Morocco.
Marty, Colonel, 14 January 1924.
Debas, Chef de bataillon, 25 July 1925.
Gémeau, Lieutenant-colonel breveté, 1 January 1926.
Debas, Lieutenant-colonel, 1 July 1928.
Richert, Lieutenant-colonel, 10 May 1930.
Gérard, 13 July 1934.
Girard, 1 July 1938.
Flan, 18 March 1940.

REGIMENT DE MARCHE D'AFRIQUE AU TONKIN

Tadieu, Lieutenant-colonel, 1886.
Lannegrace, Lieutenant-colonel, 1900.
Alix, Lieutenant-colonel, 1902–1905.

REGIMENT DE MARCHE DE MADAGASCAR

Oudri, Colonel, from the 2e Etranger, Régiment de Marche d'Afrique, 1895.
Cussac, Lieutenant-colonel, from the 2e Etranger, Régiment de Marche de la Légion à Diégo-Suarez, 1900–1902.

1er REGIMENT DE MARCHE DU 1er ETRANGER

EASTERN MOROCCO

Tahon, Lieutenant-colonel, 1913.
Théveney, Lieutenant-colonel, 1914.
Batbedat, Lieutenant-colonel, 1915–1918 (command abolished in January 1918).

1er REGIMENT DE MARCHE DU 2e ETRANGER
WESTERN MOROCCO

Brulard, Lieutenant-colonel, 20 August 1907.
Szarvas, Chef de bataillon, 20 November 1908.
Forey, Chef de bataillon, 27 July 1909, Régiment de Marche de la Légion et Zouaves.
Vandenberg, Lieutenant-colonel, 1 July 1912, Régiment de Marche du 2e Etranger.
Denis-Laroque, Chef de bataillon, 24 April 1913.
Girodon, Lieutenant-colonel, July 1913. Wounded May 1914.
Corbières, Lieutenant-colonel, January 1915.
Théveney, Lieutenant-colonel, 17 May 1916.
Tisseyre, Lieutenant-colonel, 17 November 1916 (command abolished in January 1918).

2e REGIMENT DE MARCHE DU 1er ETRANGER
FRANCE

Pein, Colonel (Moroccan intelligence), 1 September 1914–5 May 1915 (killed in action).
Cot, Lieutenant-colonel (Légion Etrangère), 8 May–11 November 1915. Moved to Régiment de Marche de la Légion Etrangère on amalgamation.

3e REGIMENT DE MARCHE DU 1er ETRANGER

Thiébault, Colonel (Gendarmerie), 4 September–20 September 1914.
Desgouilles, Lieutenant-colonel (active, Infantry), 20 November–13 August 1915 (amalgamation).

4e REGIMENT DE MARCHE DU 1er ETRANGER

Garibaldi, Lieutenant-colonel (volunteer), 1914–5 May 1915.

2e REGIMENT DE MARCHE DU 2e ETRANGER

Passard, Colonel, 2e Etranger, 1 September–10 December 1914.
Lecomte-Denis, Colonel (active, Infantry), 10 December 1914–25 September 1915.
De Lavenne de Choulot, Lieutenant-colonel (Tirailleurs), 19 October–11 November 1915 (amalgamation).

REGIMENT DE MARCHE DE LA LEGION ETRANGERE

Cot, Lieutenant-colonel (Légion Etrangère), 11 November 1915–15 February 1917.
Duriez, Lieutenant-colonel (Légion Etrangère), 15 February–17 April 1917 (killed in action).
Deville, Chef de bataillon (Légion Etrangère), 17 April–29 April 1917.
Rollet, Lieutenant-colonel (Légion Etrangère), 30 April 1917–31 December 1920.

Becomes 3e Régiment Etranger.

REGIMENT DE MARCHE D'AFRIQUE EN ORIENT

Niéger, Lieutenant-colonel (Saharans), Dardanelles, 1915.
Geay, Lieutenant-colonel, Serbia, 1916.
Romieu, Lieutenant-colonel, Macedonia, 1917–1918.

Disbanded 1 April 1943.

Infantry Regiment for Far East formed 1 July 1945.

REGIMENT DE MARCHE DE LA LEGION ETRANGERE EN EXTREME-ORIENT

Boreau de Roine, 1 July 1945.
Puvis de Chavannes, 3 July 1945.
Lorillot, 21 July 1945.

Becomes 2e Régiment Etranger d'Infanterie on 1 January 1946.

2e REGIMENT ETRANGER D'INFANTERIE

Lorillot, 21 July 1945 (from Régiment de Marche de la Légion Etrangère en Extrême-Orient).
Courcelle-Labrousse, 2 July 1947.
Nicolas, 1 November 1948.
Doynel de la Sausserie, 2 January 1949.
Thévenot, 29 March 1949.
Pelleterat de Borde, 15 February 1950.
Daigny, 15 December 1951.
Jacquot, 10 November 1953.
Goujon, 28 November 1956.
Thévenon, Colonel, 6 September 1958.
De Sèze, Colonel, 1 December 1959.
Romet, Lieutenant-colonel, 1 May 1961.
Le Vert, Lieutenant-colonel, 1 July 1963.
Kopf, Lieutenant-colonel, 1 July 1965.
De Monferrand, Lieutenant-colonel, 25 July 1967.

Temporarily disbanded 31 January 1968.

Re-formed as 2e Régiment Etranger 1 September 1972.

Servranckx, Colonel, 1 September 1972.
Gilbert, Lieutenant-colonel, 12 August 1974.
Mougin, Lieutenant-colonel, 12 August 1976.
Liège, Colonel, 12 August, 1978.

Resumes name of 2e Régiment Etranger d'Infanterie on 1 June 1980.

Roux de Montlebert, Lieutenant-colonel, 9 August 1980.
De Lajudie, Colonel, 10 August 1982.

3e REGIMENT ETRANGER D'INFANTERIE

Re-formed Régiment de Marche de la Légion Etrangère.

Rollet, Lieutenant-colonel, 1 January 1921–3 March 1925.
De Verville, Chef de bataillon (pro tem.), 4 March–11 July 1925.
François, Lieutenant-colonel, 12 July 1925–21 February 1926.
Blanc, Lieutenant-colonel, 22 February 1926–23 May 1928.
Michet de la Baume, Colonel breveté, 24 May 1928.
Brillat-Savarin, Lieutenant-colonel, 12 September 1932.
Mantoz, Colonel, 8 April–23 June 1936.
Mantoz, Colonel, beginning of 1937.
Lales, Colonel, 22 June 1939.
Lévêque, Colonel, 7 October 1941.
Lambert, Lieutenant-colonel, 24 July 1942.

Disbanded 24 June 1943.

Régiment de Marche de la Légion Etrangère formed from elements of 3e Régiment Etranger d'Infanterie and of 1e Régiment Etranger d'Infanterie de Marche.

Gentis, Colonel, 1 July 1943.
Tritschler, Colonel, 18 October 1943, died 7 February 1945.
Gaultier, Colonel, 11 December 1944.
Olie, Colonel, 11 March 1945.

Régiment de Marche de la Légion Etrangère again becomes 3e Régiment Etranger d'Infanterie on 2 July 1945.

Clément, Lieutenant-colonel, 2 December 1945.
Lehur, Colonel, 14 December 1945.
Méric, Colonel, 1 March 1947.
Royer, Lieutenant-colonel, 24 August 1947.
Simon, Lieutenant-colonel, 23 February 1948.
Constans, Colonel, October 1949.
Jacquot, Lieutenant-colonel, October 1950.
Laimay, Lieutenant-colonel, 27 February 1951.
Marguet, Lieutenant-colonel, 16 January 1953.
De Bruc de Montplaisir, 16 July 1953.
Lalande, Colonel, 1 December 1953.
Raberin, Colonel, 7 September 1954.
Thomas, Colonel, 1 July 1955.
Gaumé, Colonel, 11 July 1955.
De Corta, Lieutenant-colonel, 1 July 1958.

57 SAIDA. — 2e Etranger — Salle de café de la Coopérative

J. Geiser. phot.-Alger

Four of the Foreign Legion's principal bases in Algeria. Left: A Mounted Company forming square during battle exercises at Géryville, South Oran, c. 1902. Top: The Quartier Viénot at Sidi-bel-Abbès on Camerone Day, 1960.

Above: *Canteen in the 2nd RE's headquarters at Saïda, c. 1900. Overleaf: Fort Flatters, headquarters of the 1st CSPL in the depths of the Sahara, c. 1958.*

De Torquat de la Coulerie, Lieutenant-colonel, 29 February 1960.
Langlois, Colonel, 23 August 1960.
Mattéi, Lieutenant-colonel, 24 August 1962.
Iacconi, Lieutenant-colonel, 28 August 1964.
Letestu, Lieutenant-colonel, 5 October 1966.
Bramoullé, Lieutenant-colonel, 23 August 1969.
Charles-Dominé, Lieutenant-colonel, 2 September 1971.
Billot, Lieutenant-colonel, 26 July 1973.
Grosjean, Lieutenant-colonel, 12 August 1975.
Girard, Colonel, 1 August 1977.
Fouques-Duparc, Colonel, 30 July 1979.
Gosset, Lieutenant-colonel, 30 July 1981.
Guillot, Lieutenant-colonel, 1 August 1983.

4e REGIMENT ETRANGER D'INFANTERIE

Moroccan Battalions of the Legion at the end of the First World War.

Maurel, Colonel, 17 December 1920–30 December 1926.
Pourailly, Lieutenant-colonel, 1 January 1927.
Poupillier, Colonel, 3 May 1927–9 December 1928.
Mathieu, Colonel, 10 December 1928.
Conte, Lieutenant-colonel, 1 January 1933.
Gély, Lieutenant-colonel, 18 June 1934.
Conte, Colonel, 16 October 1934.
Gély, Lieutenant-colonel, 12 January 1935.
Conte, Colonel, 16 September 1935.
Lorillard, Lieutenant-colonel, 28 June 1936.
Gentis, Lieutenant-colonel, 27 July 1940.

Disbanded 14 November 1940.

15 August 1941, raising of a 4e Demi-Brigade de Légion Etrangère for French West Africa.

Bouty, Lieutenant-colonel, 15 August 1941.
Gentis, Lieutenant-colonel, 27 September 1941.

Becomes 1er Régiment Etranger d'Infanterie de Marche.

1er REGIMENT ETRANGER D'INFANTERIE DE MARCHE

Formed 23 March 1943.

Gentis, Lieutenant-colonel.

Disbanded 3 June 1943. Remnants become part of the Régiment de Marche de la Légion Etrangère on 1 July 1943.

4e REGIMENT ETRANGER D'INFANTERIE (MAROC)

Formed in 1946.

Laparra, Lieutenant-colonel, 16 May 1946.

Becomes 4e Demi-Brigade de la Légion Etrangère Maroc.

4e DEMI-BRIGADE DE LA LEGION ETRANGERE MAROC

Laparra, Lieutenant-colonel, 16 September 1946.

Resumes name of 4e Régiment Etranger d'Infanterie on 16 October 1948.

4e REGIMENT ETRANGER D'INFANTERIE (MAROC)

Bablon, Lieutenant-colonel, 14 November 1948.
Sourd, Lieutenant-colonel, 10 March 1951.

Disbanded 31 May 1951.

2e BATAILLON DE LA 4e DEMI-BRIGADE DE LA LEGION ETRANGERE (MADAGASCAR)

Perrin, Chef de bataillon, 28 June 1947.

4e BATAILLON DU 4e REGIMENT ETRANGER D'INFANTERIE (MADAGASCAR)

Perrin, Chef de bataillon, 16 October 1948.
Brinon, Chef de bataillon, 7 July 1949.
Royer, Lieutenant-colonel, 9 January 1950.

Disbanded as a unit of the Legion in Madagascar, 15 December 1951.

1er BATAILLON DU 4e REGIMENT ETRANGER D'INFANTERIE

Gaucher, Chef de bataillon, 1 June 1951.
Bouchon, Chef de bataillon, 2 September 1951.
Gaucher, Chef de bataillon, 17 September 1951
Gaucher, Lieutenant-colonel, 4 October 1951.
Pfirrmann, Chef de bataillon, 22 August 1952.
Dubos, Chef de bataillon, 27 January 1954.
De Hautecloque, Chef de bataillon, 16 June 1954.

4e REGIMENT ETRANGER D'INFANTERIE

Borreill, Colonel, 1 April 1955.
Lemeunier, Colonel, 1 April 1957.
Georgeon, Lieutenant-colonel, 15 March 1959.
Vadot, Lieutenant-colonel, 1 May 1961.
Brulé, Lieutenant-colonel, 30 April 1962.

Disbanded 30 April 1964.

5e REGIMENT ETRANGER D'INFANTERIE

Debas, Colonel, 1 September 1930.
Despas, Colonel, 6 April 1934.
Imhaus, Lieutenant-colonel, 22 October 1936.
Imhaus, Colonel, 3 July 1937.
De Cadoudal, Colonel, 15 June 1939.
Alessandri, Colonel, end of 1940.
Belloc, Colonel, end of 1943.

Reduced to a single battalion after the Japanese onslaught.

Binoche, Lieutenant-colonel, 1 November 1949.
Thomas, Chef de bataillon, 25 November 1950.
Thomas, Lieutenant-colonel, 1 January 1951.
Raberin, Colonel, 9 September 1951.
De Boissieu, Lieutenant-colonel, 3 November 1954.
Andolenko, Lieutenant-colonel, 1 March 1956.
Favreau, Colonel, 2 September 1958.
Pfirrmann, Lieutenant-colonel, 6 June 1960.
Bénézit, Lieutenant-colonel, 1 July 1961.
Nouguès, Lieutenant-colonel, 1 May 1963.
Desjeux, Chef de bataillon, 1 October 1963.

Disbanded 30 November 1963.

BATAILLON DE MARCHE DU 5e REGIMENT ETRANGER D'INFANTERIE

Gaucher, Chef de bataillon, 1 July 1945.

Disbanded 20 January 1947.

5e REGIMENT MIXTE DU PACIFIQUE

Formed 1 October 1963.

Nouguès, Lieutenant-colonel, 1 October 1963.
Teissèdre, Lieutenant-colonel, 1 July 1965 (pro tem.).
Desmaisons, Colonel, 4 September 1965.
Autran, Colonel, 16 September 1967.
Chadal, Colonel, 22 August 1969.
Baltzinger, Colonel, 6 August 1971.
Cholley, Colonel, 4 August 1973.
Chevallier, Lieutenant-colonel, 11 July 1975.
Cousin, Lieutenant-colonel, 12 July 1976.
Frigard, Lieutenant-colonel, 23 July 1977.
Vézio, Lieutenant-colonel, 24 July 1978.
Galtier, Lieutenant-colonel, 27 July 1979.
Jozan, Lieutenant-colonel, 29 July 1980.
Beauchesne, Lieutenant-colonel, 6 August 1981.
Mascaro, Lieutenant-colonel, 5 August 1982.
Mayer, Lieutenant-colonel, 6 August 1983.

6e REGIMENT ETRANGER D'INFANTERIE

Taguet, Chef de bataillon, 2 September 1939.
Imhaus, Colonel, 2 October 1939.
Barre, Lieutenant-colonel, 10 March 1940.
Delore, Lieutenant-colonel, October 1941.

Disbanded 1 January 1942.

6e REGIMENT ETRANGER D'INFANTERIE

Re-formed.

Babonneau, Lieutenant-colonel, 1 April 1949.
Rossi, Lieutenant-colonel, 16 September 1952.
Georgeon, Chef de bataillon, 12 June 1954.

Disbanded 1 July 1955.

11e REGIMENT ETRANGER D'INFANTERIE

Maire, Colonel, October 1939.
Robert, Colonel, 24 December 1939.
Clément, Chef de bataillon, June 1940.

12e REGIMENT ETRANGER D'INFANTERIE

Besson, Lieutenant-colonel, February 1940.

21e REGIMENT DE MARCHE DE VOLONTAIRES ETRANGERS

Debuissy, Lieutenant-colonel.

22e REGIMENT DE MARCHE DE VOLONTAIRES ETRANGERS

Villiers-Morriamé, Lieutenant-colonel.

23e REGIMENT DE MARCHE DE VOLONTAIRES ETRANGERS

Aumoitte, Lieutenant-colonel.

13e DEMI-BRIGADE DE LA LEGION ETRANGERE

Guéninchault, Chef de bataillon, 20 February 1940 (killed in action).
Magrin-Vernerey, Lieutenant-colonel, 27 February 1940.
Amilakvari, Lieutenant-colonel, 1 October 1941 (killed in action).
Bablon, Chef de bataillon, 24 October 1942.
Arnault, Chef de bataillon, 17 October 1944.
Saint-Hillier, Lieutenant-colonel, 25 March 1945.
Bablon, Lieutenant-colonel, 1 January 1946.
De Sairigné, Lieutenant-colonel,

21 August 1946 (killed in action).
Arnault, Lieutenant-colonel, 4 March 1948.
Morel, Lieutenant-colonel, 1 April 1949.
Clément, Lieutenant-colonel, 10 April 1951.
Guigard, Lieutenant-colonel, 1 September 1952.
Gaucher, Lieutenant-colonel, 1 September 1953 (killed in action).
Lemeunier, Lieutenant-colonel, 19 March 1954.
Rossi, Lieutenant-colonel, 13 May 1954.
Marguet, Lieutenant-colonel, 30 April 1956.
Sengès, Lieutenant-colonel, 6 January 1957.
Roux, Colonel, 8 December 1958.
Vaillant, Colonel, 1 February 1961.
Dupuy de Quérézieux, Colonel, 12 July 1961.
Lacôte, Lieutenant-colonel, 24 August 1963.
Geoffrey, Chef de bataillon, 13 May 1965.
Geoffrey, Lieutenant-colonel, 1 October 1965.
Foureau, Lieutenant-colonel, 13 July 1968.
Buonfils, Lieutenant-colonel, 13 July 1970.
Pétré, Lieutenant-colonel, 17 July 1972.
Lardry, Lieutenant-colonel, 12 August 1974.
Coullon, Lieutenant-colonel, 16 August 1976.
Gillet, Colonel, 17 August 1978.
Loridon, Lieutenant-colonel, 17 August 1980.
Vialle, Lieutenant-colonel, 18 August 1982.

1er REGIMENT ETRANGER DE CAVALERIE

Perret, Colonel, 8 March 1921.
Sala, Lieutenant-colonel, 28 April 1922.
Maurel, Colonel, 19 February 1923.
Sala, Colonel, 23 January 1925.
Burnol, Colonel, 3 December 1931.
Bonnefous, Colonel, 1 May 1932.
Berger, Colonel, 8 November 1935.
Levavasseur, Colonel, 11 June 1940.
Miquel, Colonel, 15 September 1943.
Lennuyeux, Chef d'escadrons, 17 September 1945.
Robert, Colonel, 10 October 1945.
Marion, Lieutenant-colonel, 21 August 1946.
Doré, Lieutenant-colonel, 14 June 1948.
De Battisti, Lieutenant-colonel, 10 May 1949.
Royer, Lieutenant-colonel, 17 April 1951.
Deluc, Lieutenant-colonel, 1 November 1952.
Hardoin, Lieutenant-colonel, 5 April 1953.
Coussaud de Massignac, Lieutenant-colonel, 30 August 1954.
Ogier de Baulny, Chef d'escadrons, 28 May 1956.

Spitzer, Lieutenant-colonel, 1 August 1956.
De Blignières, Lieutenant-colonel, 15 August 1958.
De la Chapelle, Lieutenant-colonel, 23 August 1960.
Barazer de Lannurien, Lieutenant-colonel, 9 June 1961.
De Monplanet, Lieutenant-colonel, 30 April 1962.
De Froissard de Broissia, Lieutenant-colonel, 1 August 1963.
Ansoborlo, Lieutenant-colonel, 30 October 1965.
Bart, Lieutenant-colonel, 26 September 1967.
Caillard d'Aillières, Lieutenant-colonel, 13 September 1969.
Fesneau, Lieutenant-colonel, 18 September 1971.
Lorho, Lieutenant-colonel, 1 September 1973.
Devouges, Lieutenant-colonel, 1 September 1975.
Le Corre, Lieutenant-colonel, 2 September 1977.
Audemart d'Alançon, Lieutenant-colonel, 1 September 1979.
De La Presle, colonel, 2 September 1981.
Ansart de Lessan, Lieutenant-colonel, 1 October 1983.

2e REGIMENT ETRANGER DE CAVALERIE

Farine, Colonel, 1 July 1939.
Billon, Chef d'escadrons, 16 September 1940.
Billon, Chef d'escadrons, 21 September 1940 (provisional, until disbandment in 1940).

Disbandment, then reorganization of the Regiment in 1946.

Lennuyeux, Lieutenant-colonel, 1946.
De Chazelles, Lieutenant-colonel, 7 August 1948.
Berchet, Lieutenant-colonel, 1 April 1952.
Renucci, Lieutenant-colonel, 19 January 1953.
Legendre, Lieutenant-colonel, 12 January 1955.
Ogier de Baulny, Colonel, 18 January 1957.
De Coatgoureden, Lieutenant-colonel, 17 January 1960.
Baldini, Lieutenant-colonel, 3 August 1961.

Disbanded 31 July 1962.

97e GROUPE DE RECONNAISSANCE DIVISIONNAIRE

Lacombe de la Tour, Lieutenant-colonel, 3 February 1940 (killed in action).
De Guiraud, Capitaine, 11 June 1940.

GROUPE AUTONOME DU REGIMENT ETRANGER DE CAVALERIE

TUNISIA, 1943

Royer, Chef d'escadrons.

1er BATAILLON ETRANGER DE PARACHUTISTES

Segrétain, Capitaine, 1 July 1948 (killed in action).
Raffalli, Capitaine, 16 October 1950.
Vieules, Capitaine, 22 November 1950.

Disbanded 1 January 1951 and reorganized 18 March 1951.

Darmuzai, Capitaine, 18 March 1951.
Brothier, Chef de bataillon, 21 June 1952.
Guiraud, Capitaine, 10 April 1953.
Chalony, Capitaine, 17 May 1954.
Denoix de Saint-Marc, Capitaine, 12 July 1954.
Germain, Capitaine, 24 July 1954.
Jeanpierre, Chef de bataillon, 1 November 1954.

1er REGIMENT ETRANGER DE PARACHUTISTES

Jeanpierre, Chef de bataillon, 1 September 1955.
Brothier, Lieutenant-colonel, 4 February 1956.
Jeanpierre, Lieutenant-colonel, 25 March 1957 (killed in action 29 May 1958).
Brothier, Colonel, 1 July 1958.
Dufour, Lieutenant-colonel, 1 May 1959.
Guiraud, Lieutenant-colonel, 12 December 1960.

Disbanded 30 April 1961.

2e BATAILLON ETRANGER DE PARACHUTISTES

Solnon, Chef de bataillon, 5 November 1948.
Dussert, Capitaine, 30 October 1950.
Raffalli, Chef d'escadrons, 22 November 1950 (killed in action).
Bloch, Chef de bataillon, 1 September 1952.
Merglen, Capitaine, 30 June 1953.
Liesenfelt, Chef de bataillon, 5 October 1953.
Vial, Capitaine, 17 May 1954.
Masselot, Chef de bataillon, 1 June 1954.

2e REGIMENT ETRANGER DE PARACHUTISTES

De Vismes, Lieutenant-colonel, 1 December 1955.
Lefort, Colonel, 7 April 1958.
Darmuzai, Lieutenant-colonel, 31 March 1960.
Chenel, Lieutenant-colonel, 4 May 1961.
Caillaud, Lieutenant-colonel, 29 May 1963.
Arnaud de Foiard, Lieutenant-colonel, 21 June 1965.

Lacaze, Lieutenant-colonel, 18 July 1967.
Dupoux, Lieutenant-colonel, 8 August 1970.
Goupil, Lieutenant-colonel, 3 August 1972.
Brette, Lieutenant-colonel, 29 June 1974.
Erulin, Lieutenant-colonel, 9 July 1976.
Roue, Lieutenant-colonel, 26 July 1978.
Guignon, Lieutenant-colonel, 26 July 1980.
Janvier, Lieutenant-colonel, 31 July 1982.

DEPOT COMMUN DES REGIMENTS ETRANGERS

Azan, 30 October 1933.
Théraube, Chef de bataillon, 1 September 1935.
Azan, February 1938.
Flan, 23 April 1939.
Girard, 6 March 1940.
Bouty, 5 October 1940.
Lambert, 15 August 1941.
Barre, 1 October 1941.
Brisset, Lieutenant-colonel, 16 April 1943.
Vias, May 1943.
Lambert, 27 December 1943.
Gaultier, 1 January 1946.

DEPOT COMMUN DE LA LEGION ETRANGERE

Daigny, 1 September 1950.
Lemeunier, 1 August 1951.
Soulier, Chef de bataillon, 19 June 1953.
Lemeunier, 15 September 1953.
Petit, 1 November 1953.
Soulier, Chef de bataillon, 1 May 1954.
Arnault, 26 October 1954.

GROUPEMENT AUTONOME DE LA LEGION ETRANGERE

Olie, 1 September 1950.
Gardy, 1 October 1951.

GROUPEMENT DE LEGION ETRANGERE

Letestu, Colonel, 1 September 1972.
Foureau, Colonel, 1 September 1973.
Foureau, Général, 30 April 1976.
Goupil, Colonel, 1 November 1976.
Goupil, Général, 1 December 1978.
Lardry, Colonel, 20 September 1980.
Lardry, Général, 1 November 1980.
Coullon, Général, 11 October 1982.

BATAILLON DE MARCHE DE VOLONTAIRES ETRANGERS

Knocker, Chef de bataillon, Syria, 1940.

COMMANDEMENT DE LA LEGION ETRANGERE

Lennuyeux, Colonel, 1 July 1955.
Lennuyeux, Général, 1 October 1957.

INSPECTION DE LA LEGION ETRANGERE

Rollet, Général, March 1931.
Magrin-Vernerey (known as Monclar), Général, 1948.
Lennuyeux, Général, November 1957.

INSPECTION TECHNIQUE DE LA LEGION ETRANGERE

Gardy, Général, 31 July 1958.
Morel, Colonel, 1 January 1960.
Morel, Général, 1 May 1960.
Lefort, Général, 8 August 1962.

Disbanded 31 July 1964.

61e BATAILLON MIXTE GENIE-LEGION

Debent, Lieutenant-colonel, 1 January 1971 (on formation).
Bouchier, Lieutenant-colonel, 6 October 1972.
Brunet, Lieutenant-colonel, 11 October 1974.
Bissonnier, Lieutenant-colonel, 15 October 1976.
Bastian, Lieutenant-colonel, 17 October 1978.
Bironneau, Lieutenant-colonel, 17 October 1980.

Disbanded 2 November 1982.

DETACHEMENT DE LEGION ETRANGERE DES COMORES

Grandjean, Capitaine, 1 August 1973 (on formation).
Racaud, Lieutenant-colonel, 26 July 1975.

Becomes Détachement de Légion Etrangère de Mayotte, 1 April 1976.

DETACHEMENT DE LEGION ETRANGERE DE MAYOTTE

Sarrabère, Lieutenant-colonel, 27 July 1977.
Bargoin, Lieutenant-colonel, 27 July 1979.
Paingault, Lieutenant-colonel, 27 July 1981.
Savalle, Lieutenant-colonel, 27 July 1983.

REGIMENT D'INSTRUCTION DE LA LEGION ETRANGERE

Forcin, Lieutenant-colonel, 1 September 1977 (on formation).
Jean, Lieutenant-colonel, 1 September 1979.

Becomes 4e Régiment Etranger, 1 June 1980.

4e REGIMENT ETRANGER

Latournerie, Colonel, 30 July 1981.
Colcomb, Lieutenant-colonel, 28 July 1983.

UNIFORM AND EQUIPMENT

A number of special features distinguish the Legionnaire from other members of the French army.

The White Képi
Originally, the képi cover was white, sometimes with a neck-flap, and served as protection from the sun during the hot season. As with other troops at the time, it was therefore worn only intermittently.

Around 1907, the colour was changed to khaki and the képi cover became a general article of wear for all units involved in the conquest and pacification of Morocco. In the Foreign Legion, the combination of sun and repeated washing bleached the material, making the white képi the distinctive sign and object of pride of the Legionnaire. In battle, however, it stood out as the favourite target for enemy marksmen, and the men were therefore sometimes made to dip it in coffee grounds to restore the original colour.

Until 1939, at least in Morocco, the white képi was worn in summer and the regular form (blue band over a red base) in winter.

On 14 July 1939, the Foreign Legion marched through Paris wearing the white képi. This was not only the 150th anniversary of the storming of the Bastille, but it was the first occasion on which the white képi had been officially paraded in public. Since then, *képi blanc* has been synonymous with Legionnaire throughout the world.

New recruits only receive their white képi after successfully completing their first four weeks of training.

Epaulettes
Up to 1868, the Foreign Legion wore the same epaulettes as the line infantry (red for grenadiers, pale yellow for riflemen, etc.).

In 1868, the Legion adopted the epaulettes with green shoulderstrap and red fringe that are worn today.

Abolished between 1884 and 1887 and then again in 1915, the epaulettes were restored by General Rollet in 1930, since when they have been jealously preserved while most other units have discarded them.

The Blue Waist-Sash
As early as 1882, a broad sash (of variable colour) was worn around the waist beneath the clothing as a protection against stomach ailments. Gradually, blue came to be the established colour, and the blue waist-sash, now worn over the tunic or greatcoat, became another distinctive item of Legion uniform.

The Green Tie
This became regulation wear following the appropriation of youth-camp stocks discovered by the RMLE in 1945.

The Seven-Flamed Grenade
As a badge reserved for certain élite units, the grenade was worn by the Legion from 1874 on, either on the képi or on the collar. It is now worn on the left arm by all ranks of the Legion. The grenade has gradually assumed the form

with seven flames, the outer two turned back, with the number of the regiment stamped in the centre of the bomb.

Long-Service Stripes
These are worn below the left arm-badge by NCOs and men who have completed their first contract. One, two or three chevrons indicate five, ten or fifteen years respectively.

Sous-officiers have gold stripes (or

Top: *The Foreign Legion marching through Paris for the first time wearing the white képi, 14 July 1939. Leading the contingent is Capitaine Amilakvari, who was killed in action commanding the 13th DBLE at El Himeimat in 1942.* Above: *The RMLE in the Victory parade in Paris, 1945.*

silver in the cavalry), while *hommes du rang* have green. These reenlistment chevrons should not be confused with those worn during the First World War, which represented time spent at the front.

Pioneers
On ceremonial parades, pioneers wear the 'buffalo-hide' apron (sometimes whitened) and carry an axe. Pioneers are always bearded.

Colours and Flags
The Legion's colours – green and red – derive from those of the Swiss 2nd Battalion of 1885. The flags are in the Legion colours on the obverse and in the regulation colour of the respective unit on the reverse. The obverse of the flag is divided diagonally from the top of the staff to the opposite corner, the green being nearest the staff..

The 2nd REI's present regimental colour.

Lifesize models of Legionnaires in the Foreign Legion Museum at Aubagne. Above: in 1852. Above centre: Mexico, 1863. Above right: Tonkin, 1885. Right: Mounted Company in Morocco, 1930. Far right: Saharan campaign dress in Algeria, 1954–62.

Obverse (above) *and reverse* (right) *of the Foreign Legion's first colour, presented on 24 June 1832.*

Not having the usual simple patriotism to draw on, the Foreign Legion's unique *esprit de corps* derives from deeper resources, fortified by a number of powerful traditions. These are based on four main principles:

the will to serve well
a sense of discipline and honour
pride in a task well done
the cult of remembrance.

Festivals

CAMERONE

The anniversary of the battle of Camerone (30 April 1863) marks the start of the Legion's year. Since the beginning of the present century, this day has been the occasion of great celebration wherever Legionnaires or former Legionnaires are to be found.

The ritual recitation of the battle is read out by an officer at a ceremonial parade. In the 1st RE, the artificial hand of Capitaine Danjou, recovered from the scene of the battle, is carried solemnly to the Monument to the Dead, from where it presides over the ceremony.

The day is often preceded by a vigil on the night of 29 April, which has developed from what was originally an informal camp-fire gathering to a spectacular *son et lumière* event.

The carnival festivities on the afternoon of 30 April centre round meticulously prepared displays. Officers, NCOs and men mix freely, providing the occasion for meetings, reunions and open expressions of friendship, and reinforcing those links of comradeship that are so central to the spirit of the Legion.

CHRISTMAS

Christmas, although very differently celebrated, is as important a festival for the Foreign Legion as Camerone. It is a true 'family' festival for every Legionnaire. All ranks enter enthusiastically into the traditional Christmas activities, comprising religious services, the giving of presents, crib competitions, and the Christmas Eve vigil and midnight supper.

Immense effort is put into the decoration of barrack rooms, and great rivalry goes into the secret preparation of magnificent Christmas cribs, which are judged at the section, service or sometimes company level.

The distribution of gifts by the company commander usually takes place at an evening party attended by all those not on duty. Sketches (sometimes carefully rehearsed, sometimes improvised) are performed as part of the entertainment that continues throughout the communal midnight supper.

NEW YEAR'S DAY

The *sous-officiers* extend their New Year greetings to the officers and invite them to their mess or *popote*.

EPIPHANY

It is the turn of the officers to entertain the *sous-officiers* on the Feast of the Epiphany (6 January).

A 'king' is designated, usually a *sous-officier* chosen for his outstanding personal qualities. He appoints his 'court' and delivers a witty but tactful speech (prepared in collaboration with the commanding officer or his deputy), recounting the trivia of the past year. It is customary for the commanding officer to be made the highest personage in the 'realm' after the king, so that he can give the benefit of his advice and experience.

Either at the request of his courtiers or on his own account, the king may proclaim a number of more or less ridiculous regulations governing his court, providing only that these do not affect the sacrosanct time off-duty and extra quarter-litre of wine granted to all his subjects.

One of the king's duties on this day is to taste the soup, and he proceeds in great pomp to the kitchens to do so.

REGIMENTAL DAYS

Each regiment holds its own commemoration of one of the most notable dates in its history. The best known of these takes place on 14 September: the Fête de la Fourragère (Lanyard Festival) for the 3rd REI and the old comrades of the RMLE.

Music and Marching

CENTRAL BAND

The central band (Musique Principale de la Légion Etrangère) is attached to the 1st RE. It has earned a great reputation both for courage and for performance, and is one of the best renowned of all grand military bands. Its precise composition is fixed in detail by ministerial decree.

The band normally parades with ninety musicians, and it differs from other French bands in the following particulars:

its fifes
its 'Chinese pavilion' percussion
the carriage of the drums, with the lower circle at knee level
its marching rhythm.

THE LEGION STEP

The French infantry marches at 120 paces to the minute (double time). This was not always the case, since up to about 1830 (and specifically in the Hohenlohe Regiment) the step was much slower. It was probably from that regiment that the Foreign Legion inherited the marching tradition that gives it a special place in processional parades.

The exact rate has varied at different periods. It is now generally agreed to be eighty-eight paces to the minute.

LE BOUDIN

This is the title of the Foreign Legion's famous marching song. Both the meaning of the word and the theme of the song itself have been the cause of much confusion. In all probability, *boudin* (whose first meaning is 'black pudding') refers to the sausage-shaped tent-roll carried on the Legionnaires' back-pack.

Le Boudin

(Chorus)
Tiens, voilà du boudin, voilà du boudin,
*   voilà du boudin*
Pour les Alsaciens, les Suisses et les
*   Lorrains,*
Pour les Belges, il n'y en a plus, pour les
*   Belges, il n'y en a plus,*
Ce sont des tireurs au cul;
Pour les Belges, il n'y en a plus, pour les
*   Belges, il n'y en a plus,*
Ce sont des tireurs au cul.

—

Nous sommes des dégourdis, nous sommes
*   des lascars,*
Des types pas ordinaires,
Nous avons souvent notre cafard,
Nous sommes des Légionnaires.

Au Tonkin, la Légion immortelle
A Tuyen Quang illustra notre Drapeau.
Héros de Camerone et frères modèles
Dormez en paix dans vos tombeaux.

Nos anciens ont su mourir
Pour la Gloire de la Légion,
Nous saurons bien tous périr
Suivant la tradition.

Au cours de nos campagnes lointaines,
Affrontant la fièvre et le feu,
Nous oublions avec nos peines
La mort qui nous oublie si peu
Nous, la Légion.

It is impossible to render the full significance of these words into English, but the following more or less literal translation provides an approximation:

(Chorus)
Well, there's 'sausage', there's 'sausage',
*   there's 'sausage'*
For the Alsatians, the Swiss and the
*   Lorrainers;*
There's none left for the Belgians, there's
*   none left for the Belgians,*
They are malingerers;
There's none left for the Belgians, there's
*   none left for the Belgians,*
They are malingerers.

—

We are sharp, we are warriors,
Not ordinary fellows;
We are often bored stiff,
We are Legionnaires.

In Tonkin, the immortal Legion
Shed lustre on our Flag at Tuyen Quang.
Heroes of Camerone and model brothers,
Sleep in your tombs in peace.

Our forebears knew how to die
For the Glory of the Legion;
We shall all know how to perish,
Following tradition.

In the course of our far-off campaigns,
In the face of fever and fire,
We forget, along with our sorrows,
The death that so seldom forgets
Us, the Legion.

The origin of the music is equally obscure. It may be a melody inspired by a work of Rameau; or a theme borrowed from the song of the 67th RI in 1862; or perhaps a general tune of recognition used on the battlefield around 1840 and revived on the orders of Napoleon III. All have been suggested, but it is impossible to be certain about the precise origin. What is known is that, shortly before the Foreign Regiment's departure for Mexico, the Director of Music, Monsieur Wilhelm, based his composition of what was to become the Foreign Legion's marching song on this particular theme.

As for the words, the Legionnaires' fertile imagination seems to have given rise to many versions at different times. The present words probably originate from about 1870, when the King of the Belgians ordered his subjects not to fight in France, and when many Alsatians and Lorrainers were enlisting in the Legion.

There is no saluting during the playing of *Le Boudin*.

SALUTE TO THE CHIEF
In every regiment of the Foreign Legion, when the commanding officer arrives at the gates of any barracks or post occupied by one of his units, the guard presents arms and the bugler sounds '*Au Caïd*' ('To the Chief', *Caïd* being literally an Algerian Arab chief). Everybody hearing this must stand to attention, facing the entrance, until the end of the call.

The general commanding the GLE (the headquarters group) is greeted by the same call, followed by the first sixteen bars of *Le Boudin*.

In certain special circumstances, '*Au Caïd*' is sounded as a gesture of courtesy to a visiting dignitary who has close links with the Legion— a former commanding officer, for example.

When '*Au Caïd*' is played by drums and bugles, the drummers salute between each roll.

ROLL OF HONOUR

Between 1831 and 1983, the Foreign Legion has lost 903 officers, 3376 *sous-officiers* and 31,484 *légionnaires*, killed in the service of France.

		Officers	Sous-Officiers	Légionnaires
Algeria	1831–1882	27	61	756
Spain	1835–1839	28	98	977
Crimea	1854–1855	25	32	387
Italy	1859	4	11	128
Mexico	1863–1867	22	32	414
France	1870–1871	14	52	864
South Oran	1882–1907	8	46	601
Tonkin	1883–1910	23	159	1882
Formosa	1885	3	6	24
Dahomey	1892–1894	2	4	31
Sudan	1893–1894	–	–	2
Madagascar	1895–1901	5	27	228
Morocco	1907–1914	5	21	299
France	1914–1918	139	349	3628
Eastern Front	1914–1918	16	78	721
Morocco	1914–1918	4	40	304
Tonkin	1914–1940	1	5	49
Morocco	1920–1935	74	158	1264
Syria	1925–1927	2	6	37
World War II	1939–1945	118	821	8078
Indo-China	1945–1954	309	1082	9092
Madagascar	1947–1950	3	1	1
Tunisia	1952–1954	2	1	11
Morocco	1953–1956	3	7	56
Algeria	1954–1962	65	278	1633
Chad	1969–1970	1	–	7
Zaïre	1978	–	1	4
Chad	1978–1979	–	–	1
Lebanon	1983	–	–	5

THE LEGION'S WEAPONS

Today's Foreign Legion is armed with a number of highly specialized weapons, providing a combination of great flexibility and deadly fire-power.

5.56 mm. FA MAS Automatic Rifle

The general-issue weapon of the French Foreign Legion, classified by NATO as equivalent to the American modified M 16 A 1 rifle. The FA MAS is a personal arm, capable of firing single shots, bursts of three shots or continuous bursts, with either live ammunition or blank cartridges for training exercises. The design of the sling enables it also to be used for firing 500-gram anti-tank rounds at 65 m./sec., and anti-personnel grenades with either direct or indirect aim. The sling also enables it to be carried either on the shoulder or across the chest.

The construction is entirely of plastic and fibre-glass, giving excellent protection to the moving parts and a good grip both for firing and for carrying.

The firing mechanism lies behind the pistol-grip, inside the butt and cheek rest, while the sights are placed inside the foregrip. The rear sight has two shutters (giving three possible apertures) and can be regulated between elevations of 7 cm. and 200 m. The spring-bladed foresight can vary between 4 cm. and 200 m. Used ammunition cases can be ejected to either right or left (for the benefit of left-handed users).

Calibre: 5.56 mm.	
Weight: 4 kg.	
Length: 750 mm.	

The ammunition was adopted in 1970 from the 5.56 mm. × 45 mm. round made in 1958 for the American M 16 rifle. Its main characteristics are:

Overall width: 5.74 mm.	
Length of case: 45.5 mm.	
Weight of cartridge: 11.7 gr.	
Weight of bullet: 3.6 gr.	
Diameter of bullet: 5.69 mm.	
Diameter of case at base: 9.90 mm.	
Velocity at 100 m.: 860 m./sec.	
Velocity at 300 m.: 648 m./sec.	
Initial energy: 174 kgm.	
Energy at 100 m.: 132 kgm.	
Energy at 300 m.: 76 kgm.	
Piercing power and stopping force at 200 m. are the same as those of the NATO 7.62 mm.	

7.5 mm. Light Machine Gun, Model 1952

A general purpose, continuous-firing light machine gun, firing 7.5 mm. ammunition with truncated-cone case. It has bipod and crutch supports, with shoulder-piece, the butt set into the breech-block, and a carrying handle.

Calibre: 7.5 mm.	
Weight: 9.75 kg.	
Rate of fire: 780 rounds/minute	
Practical firing rate: 200 rounds/minute	
Maximum range: 3200 m.	
Practical range: 800 m.	
Battle sight: 600 m.	
Sight graduated from 200 m. to 2000 m.	
Penetrating power: 70 cm. of earth and 70 cm. of wood at 400 m.	
Piercing power: 12 mm. of armour plating at 100 m. (using armour-piercing ammunition)	
Magazine capacity: belts of 50 rounds, which can be joined together.	

7.5 mm. Repeating Rifle, Model F1

A weapon of very great accuracy that can be fitted either with a telescopic sight and bipod (Type A) for long-distance shooting, or with a combination of peep-hole and foresight (Type B) for medium distances. When fitted with the telescopic sight, this is the weapon of élite infantry marksmen. There is also a similar rifle of 7.62 mm. calibre.

Calibre: 7.5 mm.	
Weight (Type A): 5.07 kg.	
Weight (Type B): 4.06 kg.	
Length (without butt extension): 1138 mm.	
Ammunition: 7.5 mm. cartridge, model 1929 C.	

20 mm. Machine Cannon M 621

An automatic weapon with electrical firing mechanism, specially designed for use on light transporters (by air, land and water). This is made possible by its short recoil and relatively small size. It is flexible in use, thanks to the weapon's robustness, ease of operation and maintenance, firing mechanism and variable ammunition-feed processes. A range of ammunition can be used, according to the target.

Calibre: 20 mm.	
Weight (including cradle): 58 kg.	
Length (including cradle): 2207 mm.	
Width (including cradle): 202 mm.	
Height (including cradle): 245 mm.	
Recoil: +50 mm., −17 mm.	
Firing voltage: 250 V.	
Rate of fire: 740 or 300 rounds/minute	
Firing technique: single shots, limited or unlimited bursts.	

Milan Anti-Tank Weapon

The most effective of all infantry anti-tank weapons, with unrivalled firepower and range for such a light weapon. Because of its handiness and lack of bulk, it is normally used from the ground, but can also be fitted to various types of vehicle. The missile is fired directly from the tube in which it is transported and stored. This is placed on the launching block, which contains the priming mechanism, visual and infra-red sights, and remote control system. The firing position is from a tripod mounting or from against the shoulder with a rest. The missile is kept on line by wire-guided remote control, operated by simply keeping the infra-red sight on the target throughout its flight. At short range, the Milan can be used like an ordinary rocket-launcher, making it effective from 25 m. to 2000 m. Its accuracy against stationary or moving vehicles, amoured or not, at close quarters or medium range, is thus unaffected by distance.

Weight (with missile, ready to fire): 11.3 kg.	
Weight (in tactical packing): 11.8 kg.	
Weight (with launching block and tripod): 17 kg.	
Velocity: 210 m./sec. at 2000 m.	
Range: 25 m. to 2000 m.	
Piercing power: three times NATO 'heavy tank' target	
Propulsion: gas generator from tube	
Guidance: automatic wire-guided remote control.	

89 mm. Anti-Tank Rocket Launcher (LRAC), Model F1

A lightweight anti-tank weapon that can be operated by one man, but more usually by two (a gunner and a loader). The hollow charge has expanding fins. At the moment of firing, the rocket packing is fixed to the launch tube.

Calibre: 89 mm.	
Weight (with telescopic sight): 5 kg.	
Length: 1170 mm.	
Weight (with missile, ready to fire): 8 kg.	
Length (with missile, ready to fire): 1600 mm.	
Piercing power: 400 mm. of armour plating 1000 mm. of concrete	
Practical range: 300 m. at moving target	
Distribution: 1 LRAC per combat group 5 LRACs per combat section 10 rockets per weapon.	

Top: *5.56 mm. FA MAS automatic rifle.* Above: *7.5 mm. light machine gun.*

FAMOUS LEGIONNAIRES

A number of men, better known in other walks of life, have also served in the ranks of the Legion.

PATRICE DE MACMAHON. Duke of Magenta, Marshal of France, President of France (1873–79). Lieutenant-colonel commanding 2nd Foreign Regiment, 1843–44.

VITALIS PASHA. Turkish general. Military commander of Eastern Rumelia. Légionnaire, lieutenant and capitaine in Foreign Regiment, 1844–68.

CAPITAINE BONAPARTE. Grandson of Lucien Bonaparte (brother of Napoleon). Capitaine in Foreign Regiment in Mexico, 1863–67.

PETER I. King of Serbia (1903–21). Served as Sous-lieutenant Kara [georgevich] in Foreign Regiment, 1870.

JOSEPH SCHNEIDAREK. Czech general. Military governor of Prague (1919), military commander of Eastern Slovakia and Carpathian Ruthenia (1925). Légionnaire and caporal in 2nd Foreign Regiment, 1900–05.

ERNST JÜNGER. German expressionist writer. Légionnaire in 1st Foreign Regiment, 1913.

EDOUARD DALADIER. French statesman. Holder of many ministerial posts (1924–40), Prime Minister (1933, 1934, 1938–40). Sergent-vaguemestre (baggage-master) in 2nd Marching Regiment of the 1st Foreign Regiment, 1914–15.

BLAISE CENDRARS. Swiss-born French novelist and poet. Caporal in Foreign Legion Marching Regiment, 1914–16. Lost an arm, awarded Military Medal.

ALAN SEEGER. American poet. Enlisted in 1914, caporal in Foreign Legion Marching Regiment. Killed in battle at Belloy-en-Santerre, 1916.

FRANÇOIS FABER. Luxembourg cycling champion. Winner of Tour de France (1909) and Bordeaux–Paris race (1911). Caporal in Foreign Legion Marching Regiment. Awarded Military Medal, killed in action, 1915.

COLE PORTER. American composer and lyricist. Légionnaire in Foreign Legion Marching Regiment, 1918.

ZINOVI PECHKOFF. Général de Corps d'Armée and French ambassador. Russian-born adopted son of Maxim Gorky, the famous writer. Légionnaire in Foreign Legion Marching Regiment in World War I, lost an arm, awarded Military Medal. Commissioned as officer after the war, capitaine and chef de bataillon in the Legion in Morocco and Spain until 1938.

LOUIS II. Prince of Monaco (1922–49).

Général de Division. Chef de bataillon in 1st Foreign Regiment between the two World Wars.

AAGE OF DENMARK. Danish Prince. Great-great-grandson of Louis-Philippe, creator of the Foreign Legion. Capitaine and chef de bataillon in 2nd and 3rd Foreign Infantry Regiments, 1922–40.

BORIS KRESHATITSKY. Brigadier-general in Russian Imperial Army. Légionnaire and lieutenant in 1st Foreign Cavalry Regiment in Morocco and Syria, 1925–40.

ALI KHAN. Son of Aga Khan III. Lieutenant in 1st and 6th Foreign Regiments in Syria, 1938–39.

DAVID SHALTIEL. Israeli general, commander-in-chief of Jewish forces in Jerusalem (1948). Sergent in Foreign Legion during World War II.

PRINCE NAPOLEON. Bonaparte pretender to the French throne. Légionnaire in 1st Foreign Regiment (Dépôt Commun des Régiments Etrangers), under name of Blanchard, 1940.

ARTHUR KOESTLER. Hungarian-born English writer and philosopher.

Légionnaire in 1st Foreign Regiment, 1940.

COUNT OF PARIS. Orleanist pretender to the French throne. Direct descendant of Louis-Philippe, creator of the Legion. Légionnaire in 1st Foreign Regiment, under name of d'Orliac, 1940–41.

HANS HARTUNG. German-born French abstract painter. Légionnaire in 1st Foreign Regiment, 1940–42.

PIERRE MESSMER. French statesman. Minister of Defence and Prime Minister under Presidents de Gaulle and Pompidou. Lieutenant and capitaine in 13th Foreign Legion Half-Brigade, 1940–45.

FERNAND GRAVEY. Belgian-born French actor and film producer. Légionnaire in Foreign Legion Marching Regiment, 1944–45.

FREDERIC ROSSIF. Italian-born French film producer. Légionnaire in 13th Foreign Legion Half-Brigade 1944–45.

GIUSEPPE BOTTAI. Italian politician. Minister of Education and Religious Affairs under Mussolini. Maréchal des logis in 1st Foreign Cavalry Regiment, under name of Battaglia, 1944–48.

Sous-lieutenant Georges Kara, the name adopted by Prince Karageorgevich (the future King Peter I of Serbia) when serving in the Foreign Regiment in 1870.

NATIONALITIES IN THE FOREIGN LEGION

As its name suggests, the Foreign Legion's primary concern has been the recruitment of foreigners. However, from the very outset, there have always been Frenchmen in its ranks.

The percentage of each nationality has fluctuated with Europe's political upheavals. The revolutionary fervour of 1830 brought numerous refugees to France—Spaniards caught up in liberal agitation; Italians fleeing the duchies of Parma and Modena; francophile Germans from Saxony, Hanover and the Rhineland; Belgians seeking a national identity; Polish survivors of the Russian repression that followed the Warsaw rising. The organization of battalions by nationalities gives a good indication of these origins:

1st, 2nd and 3rd Battalions—Swiss and Germans
4th Battalion—Spaniards
5th Battalion—Sardinians and Italians
6th Battalion—Belgians and Dutch
7th Battalion—Poles.

Up until 1870, the distribution of nationalities (almost exclusively European) hardly varied at all. In 1863, the 3rd Company of the Foreign Regiment, which had fought the historic battle of Camerone in Mexico, comprised the following nationalities, in order of numerical importance:

Germans, Belgians, French, Swiss, Italians, Spaniards, Dutch, Danes and Austrians.

Between 1870 and World War I, there was a high proportion of Alsatians and Lorrainers, resulting from the German annexation of their lands. It is interesting to note that, when recruitment from Alsace and Lorraine was at its height, German enlistment first diminished but then increased again.

Nationalities in 1896/1897

Alsace-Lorrainers	2635
Germans	2511
French	1805
Belgians	1712
Swiss	975
Austrians	353
Spaniards	81
British	56
Turks	46

with small numbers of Poles, Luxemburgers, Czechs, Hungarians, Greeks and Russians.

Nationalities on 1 January 1913

French	45.2%
Germans	17.6%
Belgians	7.4%
Alsace-Lorrainers	6.7%
Swiss	5.9%
Italians	4.5%
Spaniards	2.5%
Russians	1.1%
Luxemburgers	0.7%
Tunisians, Moroccans, Austrians, Dutch, Americans, Hungarians, Turks	1.7%
Others	6.7%

out of an overall total of 10,521 men.

The period 1914–18 saw massive enlistment of foreigners from all parts of the world: aliens resident in France, allies cut off from their own armies, and others from neutral countries rallying to the cause of freedom. At this time, the Legion contained more than a hundred nationalities. The detailed analysis of nationalities (although plainly carried to extremes, particularly with regard to colonial origins) was recorded in *Le Livre d'Or du RMLE, 1914–1918* as follows:

Abyssinians		3
Albanians		6
Algerians		500
Alsace-Lorrainers		2583
Americans		600
Annamese		10
Argentines		109
Armenians		71
Australians		8
Austrians		1270
Belgians		1721
Bolivians		5
Brazilians		79
British		252
Bulgarians		44
Cambodians		4
Canadians		26
Chileans		28
Chinese		5
Cochin-Chinese		4
Colombians		12
Congolese		2
Costa Ricans		2
Cubans		26
Cypriots		2
Czechs		524
Dahomeyan		1
Danes		85
Dutch		215
Ecuadorians		3
Egyptians		88
Filipinos		23
French		6239
Gabonese		2
Gambian		1
Germans		3087
Gibraltarian		1
Greeks	(see also below)	2486
Guadeloupians		3
Guatemalans		3
Guianese, British		1
Guianese, French		1
Guineans, French		5
Guineans, Portuguese		2
Haitians		21
Hindus, British		12
Hindus, Dutch		2
Hong Kong		1
Indo-Chinese		10
Italians		6402
Ivorians		2
Jamaicans		3
Japanese	(see also below)	60
Libyans		4
Luxemburgers		624
Madagascans		20
Maltese		13
Martiniquais		1
Mauritanian		1
Mauritians		18
Mexicans		21
Monegasques		20
Montenegrins	(see also below)	61
Moroccans		133
New Caledonians		8
New Zealander		1
Nicaraguans		6
North African		1
Norwegians		33
Panamanian		1
Paraguayan		1
Persians		13
Peruvians		13
Poles		749
Portuguese		86
Puerto Ricans		4
Réunionais		3
Romanians		758
Russians		5242
Saint Lucian		1
Saint Pierre and Miquelon		3
Salvadorians		6
Senegalese		22
Serbs		115
Siamese		2
Somalian		1
Spaniards		1996
Sudanese		10
Swedes		65
Swiss		2752
Syrians		75
Tonkinese		4
Transvaalers		4
Tunisians		171
Turks		787
Uruguayans		21
Venezuelans		8
West Indians, British		2
West Indian, Danish		1
West Indian, French		1
Greek Battalion (arrived at the front ready-formed)		928
Japanese Detachment (arrived ready-formed)		53
Montenegrin Battalion (arrived from Serbia ready-formed)		948
Others (nationalities unclear)		417
TOTAL		**42,883**

Heads of Legionnaires. Top left: *in 1840.* Top centre: *in Kabylia, 1855.* Top right: *in France, 1870–71.* Above: *in France, 1944–45.*

Officer's, sous-officier's *and* légionnaire's *shakos in 1831.*

Two dramatic moments of the Legion's history. Top: *The 2nd RE in the assault on Zaatcha, southern Algeria, on 26 November 1849.* Above: *The death of Colonel Viénot in the trenches before Sebastopol, 2 May 1855.*

Between the two World Wars, political and economic circumstances in various countries produced their effect. From about 1920 onwards, there was heavy enlistment from the Balkans and particularly large numbers of White Russians fleeing the Soviet regime. Around 1923, Fascist rule in Italy led to increasing numbers of recruits from that country, as was the case with Germans after 1933, Spaniards in 1938, and Poles and Czechs in 1939–40.

Recruitment in 1929

Germans	1304
Franco-Belgians	717
Swiss	224
Poles	224
Italians	194
Russians	128
Czechs	88
Austrians	78
Balkans	61
British	45
Luxemburgers	38
Dutch	24
Scandinavians	19
Turks, Syrians, Egyptians, Armenians, North Africans	38
TOTAL	3182

Recruitment in 1934

Germans	375
French	203
Belgians	91
Poles	81
Italians	71
Swiss	30
Hungarians	30
Czechs	30
Austrians	20
Spaniards	16
Luxemburgers	12
Yugoslav	1
Others (19 nationalities)	53
TOTAL	1013

Recruitment in 1935

French	815
Germans	597
Italians	308
Poles	274
Belgians	238
Swiss	143
Czechs	96
Spaniards	81
Luxemburgers	72
Austrians	50
Yugoslavs	50
Hungarians	37
Others (20 nationalities)	350
TOTAL	3111

Recruitment in 1939

Spaniards	3052

Germans	1171
Czechs	801
Belgians	779
Italians	639
Poles	615
Austrians	381
Russians	109
Luxemburgers	88
Hungarians	65
Dutch	61
Yugoslavs	60
Portuguese	49
French	48
Romanians	47
British	42
Greeks	19
Lithuanians	12
Turks	12
Danes	11
Estonians	10
Armenians	6
Americans	5
Swedes	5
Bulgarians	4
Latvians	4
Finns	3
Norwegians	3
Egyptian	1
Others	44
TOTAL	8146

After 1945, Germans formed the majority of recruits, while, for obvious geographical reasons, the largest percentages by nationality came from Western European countries—the traditional source of recruitment. Then, in the years around 1960, political events produced a significant intake from Central Europe (Hungarians, Poles and Czechs). The following statistics have been drawn up for this period:

French-speaking peoples (French, Monegasques, Belgians, Swiss, etc.)	52.0%
Germans	12.9%
Eastern Europeans	7.8%
Spaniards	7.4%
Italians	6.7%
Portuguese	3.3%
Scandinavians	2.5%
British	0.6%
Americans, Asians, Africans	6.8%

Since 1975, the number of nationalities represented in the Foreign Legion has increased from seventy to more than a hundred at the end of 1983. These can be conveniently classified into the following broad linguistic groups:

French	59%
German	12%
Italian, Spanish, Portuguese	11%
Slavonic	5%
English	3%
African and Asian	2%
Norse	1%
Others	7%

Since 1831, the strength of the Legion has varied between 3000 and 45,000. From a regular complement of about 5000 up to 1875, there was a steady increase, to 33,000 in 1932 and finally to 45,000 in 1940. In all, a total of some 600,000 rank and file have served in the Foreign Legion's regiments between 1831 and 1983. The records indicate the following approximate breakdown by country of origin since 1831, in order of numerical importance:

More than 10,000 men   Germany, Italy, Belgium, France, Spain, Switzerland, Poland
5000–10,000   Russia, Austria, Hungary, Greece, Czechoslovakia
1000–5000   Holland, Yugoslavia, Luxembourg, Great Britain, Romania, Portugal, Denmark, Turkey
100–1000   USA, Bulgaria, Finland, Sweden, Algeria, Vietnam, Morocco, Tunisia, Argentina, Brazil, Japan, Canada, Lithuania, Latvia, Norway, Egypt
20–100   More than 80 countries.

EQUIVALENT RANKS

Within the text, military ranks have been given in the French form. The table below indicates the equivalent ranks in the British and US armies.

FRENCH ARMY	BRITISH ARMY	US ARMY
Maréchal de France	Field Marshal	General of the Army
Général d'Armée	General	General
Général de Corps d'Armée	Lieutenant General	Lieutenant General
Général de Division	Major General	Major General
Général de Brigade	Brigadier	Brigadier General
Colonel	Colonel	Colonel
Lieutenant-colonel	Lieutenant Colonel	Lieutenant Colonel
Commandant	Major	Major
Capitaine	Captain	Captain
Lieutenant	Lieutenant	First Lieutenant
Sous-lieutenant	Second Lieutenant	Second Lieutenant
Aspirant	——	——
Major	——	——
Adjudant-chef	Warrant Officer I	Chief Warrant Officer
Adjudant	Warrant Officer II	Warrant Officer Junior Grade
Sergent-major (now obsolete)	——	First Sergeant
Sergent-chef	Staff Sergeant	Master Sergeant
——	——	Sergeant First Class
Sergent	Sergeant	Sergeant
Caporal-chef	——	——
Caporal	Corporal	Corporal
Soldat (légionnaire) de 1re classe	Lance Corporal	Private First Class
Soldat (légionnaire) de 2e classe	Private	Private

Exact equivalents do not always exist.

In the French army, all ranks up to caporal-chef are termed *hommes du rang*; sergent to major, *sous-officiers*; aspirant to capitaine, *officiers subalternes*; and commandant to colonel, *officiers supérieurs*. In this book, the term 'other ranks' includes both *sous-officiers* and *hommes du rang*, while 'NCOs' is used loosely for *sous-officiers*. The French form 'légionnaire' is used to indicate the rank of private soldier, while the English form 'Legionnaire' indicates membership of the Foreign Legion, irrespective of rank.

Equivalent ranks usually hold a higher command in the French army than in the British. Thus, a French three-battalion régiment (equivalent to a British brigade) is commanded by a colonel with a lieutenant-colonel as his second-in-command; a French bataillon is commanded by a commandant, or frequently by a capitaine; while the commander of a compagnie does not rank higher than lieutenant.

Maréchal des logis is used in the French cavalry instead of sergent, and brigadier in the artillery instead of caporal.

SELECT BIBLIOGRAPHY

BERGOT, Erwan. *Les 170 jours de Dien Bien Phu*, Paris, 1979.
—. *Deuxième Classe à Dien Bien Phu*, Paris, 1964, 1976.
—. *La Légion*, Paris, 1972.
—. *La Légion au Combat*, Paris, 1975.
BJORKELUND, Jan. *Legionen er Vart*, Oslo, 1981.
BLOND, Georges. *Histoire de la Légion Etrangère (1831–1981)*, Paris, 1981.
BONNECARRÈRE, Paul. *Par le Sang versé*, Paris, 1977.
BRUNON, Jean. *Camerone*, Paris, 1981.
—, et al. *Le Livre d'Or de la Légion Etrangère* (150th anniversary edition, with new chapter by T. Szecsko), Paris, Limoges, 1981.
CHARTON, Col. P. *Il y a la Légion . . .*, Paris, 1977.
CHAUVEL, Jean-François. *Kolwezi*, Paris, 1978.
CRESPO, Julio. *Por los Caminos de la Aventura*, Cochabamba (Bolivia), 1980.
EBBESON, Christian. *Fremmedlegionen*, Copenhagen, 1976.
GARROS, Louis. *Storia della Legione Straniera*, Geneva, 1972.
GAULTIER, Gen. L., and Jacquot, Col. C., *C'est la Légion*, Marseilles, 1972.
HORNUNG, Peter. *Die Legion Europas letzte Söldner*, Munich, 1981.
La Légion Etrangère a 150 ans, Aubagne, 1981.
LE MIRE, Henri. *L'Epopée moderne de la Légion, 1940–1976*, Paris, 1977.
—. *Histoire de la Légion*, Paris, 1978.
MACLEAVE, Hugh. *The Damned Die Hard*, New York, 1973.
MALCROS, Christian, and *Képi Blanc*. *Les Insignes de la Légion Etrangère*, Aubagne, 1981.
Marches et Chants de la Légion Etrangère, Aubagne, 1976.
MATTÉI, Col. A. *Tu survivras longtemps*, Paris, 1975.
MURRAY, Simon. *Legionnaire*, London, 1978.
PÉNETTEY, Gen. M., and Castaingt, Capt. J. *La Legion Extranjera en la Intervención*, Mexico City, 1962.
QURIS, Bernard. *L'Aventure Légionnaire*, Paris, 1971.
SERGENT, Pierre. *Camerone*, Paris, 1980.
—. *La Légion saute sur Kolwezi*, Paris, 1978.
—. *Les Maréchaux de la Légion*, Paris, 1977.
TURNBULL, Patrick. *The Foreign Legion*, London, 1964.
WAGNER, Otto. *S. Cizinecko Legii Proti Rommelovi*, Prague, 1970.
WELLARD, James. *The French Foreign Legion*, London, 1964.
WINDROW, Martin. *Uniforms of the French Foreign Legion 1831–1981*, London, 1981.

The Camerone memorial in Mexico, erected in 1965.

ACKNOWLEDGMENTS

Answering the phone one autumn evening in 1982, I collected my thoughts as I listened to the rapid flow of French. The caller was Colonel Forcin of the French Foreign Legion, speaking from the Legion's headquarters at Aubagne in southern France. 'I have prepared a programme for you. When can you come?' he enquired. Arrangements were made for me to arrive at the Legion's headquarters with the minimum of delay. After the call I sat back quietly, reflecting. Permission to do the book had taken so long. Months of waiting and wondering. Now I could begin.

Without the Legion's cooperation, this book would not have been possible. Permission from Paris would in itself not have secured this intimate insight into the French Foreign Legion. The Legion not only allowed me to photograph; it took me into its life and I became a guest within the 'Legion Family'. I was given total freedom to photograph where and when I wanted—within the limits of national security. The public has a confused view of the Legion, painted by poorly researched films and deserters peddling their experiences to some sensationalist newspaper. The Legion will always have its critics. However, I hope this book will at least dispel some of the myths, reveal some of its humanity and show that it is one of the élite fighting forces of the twentieth century.

In a book such as this, there is great difficulty in expressing tribute to all who have helped me along the way: from the Legionnaires who set up my jungle bivouac to the commandant, who, within a few hours, found fresh supplies of film in a remote corner of Africa, following the loss of my own on a flight from Paris. The following are but a few who gave me help, hospitality and support:
The President of France, François Mitterand, who considered my request for this book and instructed the French Ministry of Defence to give every assistance.
General J.-C. Coullon, Commander of the Legion of Honour, General Commanding the Groupement de Légion Etrangère and the 31st Brigade.
Colonel R. Forcin, Officer of the Legion of Honour and Second-in-Command of the Groupement de Légion Etrangère.
All commanding officers, officers, *sous-officiers* and légionnaires of the regiments and units I visited.

I would also like to thank Lieutenant-colonel R. Jean-Richard, Press Liaison Officer, and Commandant J.-B. Chiaroni, Editor-in-Chief of *Képi Blanc*, who were always available to arrange and assist with visits and transport to my many locations.

To Adjudant-chef T. Szecsko, Curator of the Legion Museum, and his staff at Aubagne, my gratitude for providing endless material and photographs, complete with detailed historical notes. Such tireless attention by A/C Szecsko has given great depth to the historical section of my book.

I am especially indebted to Len Deighton, who not only wrote the Introduction, but also found time to read and make valuable suggestions to my text, as well as providing constant encouragement and direction.

My appreciation also to Monsieur E. Bergot, a former Legion officer, for undertaking to write his informative and colourful historical contribution at the beginning of this book.

Maintaining a frequent dialogue with the senior officers of the Legion would have been impossible without the invaluable assistance of Madame Michelle Rover, who acted as my interpreter and secretary during many complex negotiations, regardless of the day or hour.

Finally, to my wife Jennifer, who spent endless days and nights editing thousands of transparencies, arranging finance, transport, hotels, inoculations and the innumerable other tasks which are necessary for a photographer embarking on a project such as *The French Foreign Legion*. Without her relentless devotion in all these areas, and her being there when needed, this book could not have been created.

The author and publisher are deeply indebted to the Service Information et Historique de la Légion Etrangère (SIHLE) and *Képi Blanc* (the official review of the Foreign Legion) for their invaluable contribution to the book. Apart from the information on Equivalent Ranks (page 209), the SIHLE provided the complete documentation on which the section entitled 'The Military Background' is based. The table of Equivalent Ranks is extracted from material supplied by the Army Attaché at the French Embassy in London, while the explanatory note was kindly contributed by Lt Colonel Patrick Turnbull. The list of Commanding Officers 1831–1983 (pages 187–196) and the Roll of Honour (page 201) are reprinted (with additions) from *Le Livre d'Or de la Légion Etrangère* (150th anniversary edition, published by Charles-Lavauzelle, Paris and Limoges, 1981) by kind permission of Monsieur Raoul Brunon and the publisher.

All the illustrations in 'The History of the Legion' and 'The Military Background' (except for the two on page 203), as well as those on pages 1, 4 and 6, are from the Foreign Legion's own photographic archives, and are reproduced by courtesy of *Képi Blanc*. All other photographs are by John Robert Young.

The paintings and drawings reproduced in the book are by the following artists: J.-A. Beaucé, 15 (top); P. Benigni, 6, 11, 12, 13, 14 (top and bottom), 19 (bottom), 22 (bottom), 26, 30 (top), 178 (top and bottom), 179, 182, 183 (bottom left); C.-J. Hallo, 35; J. Mevet, 23 (right); A. Rosenberg, 10 (bottom), 22 (top), 23 (centre), 30 (bottom), 34 (bottom right), 206 (4 x); L. Rousselot, 18 (top), 207 (top and bottom); Talpach, 187; M. Toussaint, 21, 27, 28 (top).

PHOTOGRAPHY NOTES

Simplicity is everything. Over the years, I have constantly reminded myself to reduce a problem to its lowest common denominator—whether it be the assignment, equipment or travel. The reason for being at a particular location is to interpret visually what is around you and, as a photo-journalist, to maintain a low profile. I always keep equipment to a minimum—especially when travelling out of Britain. Airport security is always a problem and excessive amounts of equipment do not endear you to security and customs officials. Film stock is another problem, as I usually carry about 150 rolls on each trip. Contrary to what officials may tell you, X-ray machines and film are poor travelling companions. Consequently, film stock is packed with my personal baggage and put in the plane's cargo hold. Even then it can be lost—which happened on my Djibouti trip. For some years I have used Leica, Leicaflex S/L and R3 and recently R4 cameras, with a series of lenses from 19 mm. to 180 mm. The Leitz lenses are superb, as the colour plates in the book demonstrate. When travelling, I try to keep to two bodies and six lenses. If the region is particularly remote, like my trip into the jungle of French Guiana, a third body will be carried. All the equipment is packed into a battered metal case, with a stout carrying handle, and fits snugly under most airline seats. Depending on where I am working, I carry one of several soft bags, which I work from in the field. It is capable of carrying two bodies and four lenses, together with some thirty rolls of film. My favourite is an old shopping bag, fitted with a waterproof lining and handles long enough to carry over my shoulder. The metal case also contains: watchmaker's screwdrivers, a collection of chamois leathers (ideal for wrapping lenses and camera bodies), a Swiss army knife, and brushes for cleaning, purchased at the local paint or hardware shop. A light meter and several polarizing filters complete the outfit.

SOME STATISTICS OF INTEREST

Research before photography commenced: one year.
Photography: commenced October 1982; completed November 1983.
Locations: Southern France—Aubagne, Orange and Castelnaudary.
Corsica—Calvi and Bonifacio.
South America—French Guiana.
Africa—Djibouti and Algeria.
Distance travelled: more than 50,000 miles.
Transport: car, jeep, civilian and military aircraft, military helicopter, pirogue and a lot of walking.
Film stock used: 310 rolls, providing over 3000 transparencies, from which the final selection of about 150 was made. This library of photographs of the Foreign Legion is one of the most comprehensive outside the French Ministry of Defence.
Film editing time: more than 700 hours.